Wit & Wisdom of AFRICA

PROVERBS from AFRICA & the CARIBBEAN

PATRICK IBEKWE

Wit & Wisdom of Africa
Proverbs from Africa and the Caribbean

First published in the UK in 1998 by
New Internationalist Publications Ltd
55 Rectory Road
Oxford OX4 1BW
England

Cover photo: Woman in Burkino Faso *Claude Sauvageot*

Editor: Troth Wells
Design by New Internationalist Publications Ltd
Website – http://www.newint.org/

Printed in the United Kingdom by
T J International Ltd, Padstow, Cornwall

British Library Cataloguing-in-Publication Data.
A catalogue record for this book is available from the British Library.

ISBN 1-869847-59-8 (Paperback)
ISBN 1-869847-58-X (Hardback)

Wit & Wisdom *of* AFRICA

For Kalu, Chinyere, Chukwu, Ijeoma,
Mgbeke and Obike

Contents

If the lizard were good to eat,
it would not be so common
– **HAITIAN**

Introduction

I HAVE long been interested in and derived a great deal of pleasure from reading proverbial and aphoristic literature, with its fascinating combination of pith and point. The difference between the two forms is essentially one of provenance. Proverbs and aphorisms may be described as terse, general statements, often using figurative language, touching upon some aspect of life. But whereas the originators of aphorisms are invariably known Westerners (La Rochefoucauld, Vauvenargues, the Marquis of Halifax, Samuel Johnson, and Emerson come to mind amongst my own favourite aphorists) a proverb is a traditional saying, origination unknown,[1] which has been handed down from generation to generation as a common inheritance.

Some years ago I put down a slim collection of African proverbs I had just finished reading, and mused. I had read the collection with enjoyment, but had been struck by how easy it would have been to have improved the collection in respect of the quantity and range of the proverbs. A collection of African proverbs, it seemed to me, ought to encompass as many of the myriad cultures of that continent as possible; and while it would probably be impossible to include proverbs from every one of the hundreds of cultural and linguistic traditions that flourish across the continent, it certainly ought to be possible to cover most of the major peoples. And surely too, the collection would have been improved with greater breadth. It didn't seem to be asking for very much: indeed, I felt that I could put together a collection along these lines myself if I seriously put my mind to it.

The present work is the fruit of putting my mind, on and off over several years, to compiling a collection of African proverbs that met the foregoing ideals. Africans, due mainly to one of the greatest crimes against humanity, the slave trade, are to be found beyond the confines of the African continent. Taking 'African' to include anyone of African descent, wherever they happened to be in the world, it seemed to me that the project could

and ought to be broadened to take in diaspora cultures. The result of including some of the proverb literature of the peoples of the African Diaspora, those descendants of Africans dispersed across the world, has been to enrich the work and to make it a truly 'African' collection. And so my project assumed its final form: a collection of proverbs traversing Africa, the Caribbean and the Americas and running to several thousand proverbs.

The scope and nature of the collection

There are several unavoidable gaps in the collection. For example, as the compilation is based on English language collections of various national proverbs, I have been confined in my choice of material to what is available in that language. Many traditions have not been compiled in English, or exist in English but are unknown to me and my research, or have not been compiled at all in English or the indigenous language in question. Thus, for example, there are no proverbs in the pages that follow for such important traditions as the Afro-Brazilian and Afro-Cuban, or for the less well-known community of Asians who had lived in Africa. And while proverbs of several Caribbean peoples do feature in the collection, as many do not for lack - as far as my researches have been able to determine - of any collections of this aspect of their folklore.

Intentionally omitted are those cultural traditions which, though present in Africa, can more properly be classed with non-African traditions. Thus Afrikaans, French, English and Portuguese proverbs would sit more naturally in a collection devoted to proverbs from Europe and the European Diaspora, while the Arabic proverbs of the Muslim peoples of North Africa are equally removed from the indigenous cultural traditions of the continent, even if their presence in Africa is of longer standing than even the European traditions just noted. The East African Swahili culture absorbed Arabic influences, but Swahili is an African language.

The collection is marked by certain factors.

To my knowledge it is the only compilation of its kind that includes some proverbs from Ancient Egypt, a culture whose antecedent links to the classical civilizations of the Mediterranean are well known, but whose irredeemably African basis and character seems to be rarely acknowledged or treated.[2] I see part of the value of the collection as lying in its juxtaposition of different but related traditions, enabling the reader to trace possible correspondences between languages belonging to the same linguistic family (for example, the Bantu languages Zulu, Sotho and Shona), or to detect parallels between a particular African culture and its putative cultural offspring half a world away (for example various West African traditions and those of the Caribbean). Of course, to establish such connections beyond all doubt would require an anthropological and linguistic investigation outside the scope of the present work, but to detect and conjecture about such possible linkages is open to any reader.

The nature of African proverbs

This collection is not an academic study of the proverbs of Africa and the African Diaspora. Readers interested in a scholarly examination of proverbs are advised to turn to the thorough and insightful work by Monye in this connection and its extensive bibliography.[3]

Instead it is an attempt to represent '... the wit, wisdom, and imagination of which [those cultures] are full... the amusement, instruction, insight into matters the most important, which they are capable of yielding.'[4] In many societies, but particularly in African ones (where traditional values and ways of living have not suffered the same degree of dislocation that has afflicted many communities of the Diaspora and elsewhere) proverbs – like tales, sagas, prayers, ritual invocations, songs, riddles, legends, spells and other folklore artefacts – have a deep cultural significance.

They provide standards against which to gauge conduct, precepts of behaviour (One who reminds the orphan of his misery makes him cry, even if it is done with kind compassion – GANDA); an index of societal and political values, means of expressing - sometimes with the most delicate tact - criticism (Blind man see him neighbour fault – JAMAICAN); and regulating social intercourse (A mouth which is harsh has no relatives – MAMPRUSSI). In brief, proverbs are an expression of a people's conception of themselves, of their values, and of their attitude to life. These proverbs, I hope, provide a window on African humanity, on and beyond the continent.

Proverbs generally, but especially in Africa, may be described as a dialectic of wisdom. They are often employed to deliver arguments in debate, to settle problems, to uncover the truth, to deliver advice, to offer observations, and to arrive at judgements on the application of customary and unwritten laws. Proverbs are also used ornamentally, to heighten and add to the artfulness of conversation, employing as they do such linguistic and literary resources as irony, humour, emphasis, satire, understatement, sarcasm, syntactical manipulation, parallelism, and so on.

The following brief selection illustrates the range and application of proverbs:

On the nature of friendship: The truth does not spoil friendship – MANDINKA

On the appropriateness of gratitude for benefits received: Do you pick kola nuts without looking up into the tree? – BALI-NYONGA

An observation on the relationship between expectation and esteem: The bee that does not sting gains no respect – IKWERRE

A reflection on human nature and humanity: A good man also sins – FANTE

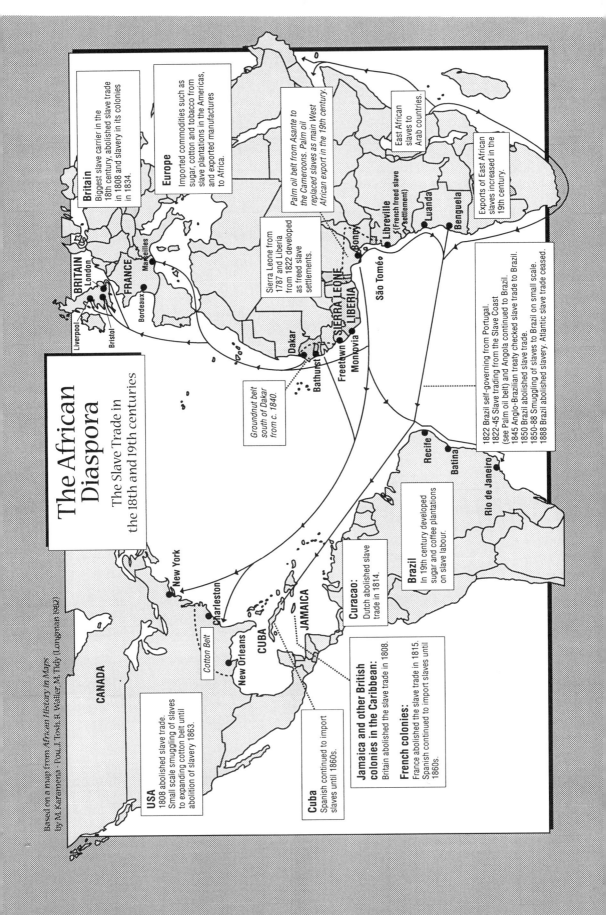

Based on a map from *African History in Maps*
by M. Katzenena · Paul J. Tosh, B. Waller, M. Tidy (Longman 1992)

The African Diaspora

The Slave Trade in
the 18th and 19th centuries

Britain
Biggest slave carrier in the 18th century, abolished slave trade in 1808 and slavery in its colonies in 1834.

Europe
Imported commodities such as sugar, cotton and tobacco from slave plantations in the Americas, and exported manufactures to Africa.

Palm oil belt from Asante to the Cameroons. Palm oil replaced slaves as main West African export in the 19th century.

East African slaves to Arab countries.

Exports of East African slaves increased in the 19th century.

Sierra Leone from 1787 and Liberia from 1822 developed as freed slave settlements.

Groundnut belt south of Dakar from c. 1840.

1822 Brazil self-governing from Portugal.
1822-45 Slave trading from the Slave Coast (see Palm oil belt) and Angola continued to Brazil.
1845 Anglo-Brazilian treaty checked slave trade to Brazil.
1850 Brazil abolished slave trade.
1850-88 Smuggling of slaves to Brazil on small scale.
1888 Brazil abolished slavery. Atlantic slave trade ceased.

Brazil
In 19th century developed sugar and coffee plantations on slave labour.

Curacao:
Dutch abolished slave trade in 1814.

Jamaica and other British colonies in the Caribbean:
Britain abolished the slave trade in 1808.

French colonies:
France abolished the slave trade in 1815. Spanish continued to import slaves until 1860s.

Cuba
Spanish continued to import slaves until 1860s.

USA
1808 abolished slave trade. Small scale smuggling of slaves to expanding cotton belt until abolition of slavery 1863.

Cotton Belt

CANADA

New York

Charleston

New Orleans

CUBA

JAMAICA

Recife

Batina

Rio de Janeiro

BRITAIN
London
Liverpool
Bristol

FRANCE
Bordeaux
Marseilles

Dakar
Bathurst
Freetown SIERRA LEONE
Monrovia LIBERIA
Bonny
São Tomé
Libreville
(French freed slave settlement)
Luanda
Benguela

A figurative expression of a particular character type: 'Im can tek milk outa kaafi. [He can take milk out of coffee, i.e. he is an especially accomplished thief] – JAMAICAN

Advice on handling others and situations: Tact removes anger from a person – OROMO

On the primacy of experience: Without tasting you can't know – BALI-NYONGA

The use of humour to lambast a serious failing (in this case laziness): You are so slow that a snake could bite you on both feet [a more energetic person would have fled after being bitten once]. – BECHUANA

On children and the need for care in their upbringing: The work of the mother appears in the child – WOLOF

On justice and patience: Nine days for the thief and one day for the owner – BALI-NYONGA.

Principles of selection

In compiling this collection, I have attempted wherever possible to exclude those proverbs that would require some elaboration of their cultural context to make their meaning clear. The proverbs that have been included are, if it can be said about any part of a living culture, self-contained and their meaning is hopefully self-evident. This, and my own preferences, have had a bearing on the selection, and means that the collection is not necessarily

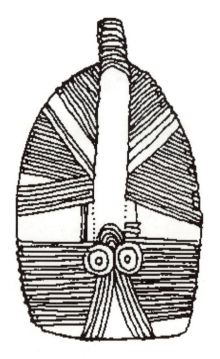

representative of the various cultures it features. It is, though, a collection of some of the most accessible, instructive and enjoyable of the proverbs of the peoples of Africa and the African diaspora.

Arrangement

Most of the proverbs in the compilation were not originally ordered under particular categories. The heads under which they are now marshalled are of my choosing, but Plissart's advice on proverbial taxonomy is worth recalling: '...the surest way of mis-interpreting the message which is being conveyed in and through proverbs is to force them into our own categories.[5] Proverbs are capable of nuances of meaning according to how and when they are used, and the fact that a proverb occurs under a particular heading is not in itself a reason for limiting the application of that proverb to that category alone. Proverbs demand consideration on the part of those who use and hear them, and a judgement on whether a particular proverb has been used pertinently and effectively. It is this interactive effort, involving sharp-witted analyses and judgements, that can make proverbs, in the mouth of a skilled proverbist, a verbal art of great fineness.

Rival proverbs

The reader will find that in many cultural traditions proverbs give contradictory advice, facing both ways on the same topic. This is sometimes used to criticize and dismiss the form. But proverbs are a reflection of life. They provide the experience of men and women, adopted and endorsed by generations who have continued to find in the wisdom of their ancestors something that touches and speaks to their own lives. Proverbs are rightly contradictory because life does not always offer a single answer to a question, if it offers an answer at all. Above all, proverbs are circumstantial: it is the situation that makes for the proverb, and circumstances, varying infinitely, draw forth an infinite variety of proverbial utterances. Thus the variety of circumstance reconciles and makes compatible the existence of two or more ostensibly contradictory sayings.

Creole English proverbs

Some proverbs from the Caribbean and the Americas are given in Creole English. I have not attempted to replace these with translations as they are the authentic voice of the peoples concerned and only in their original form is it possible to appreciate the rhythmic and aesthetic virtues many of them possess. Where the Creole terms are likely to impede the reader's ability to understand the proverbs I have either followed a proverb with a standard English version, or given (in square brackets) an explanatory word. Elsewhere in the text, words within square brackets are again intended to represent minor corrections to the grammar or spelling of the original text.

Attribution of proverbs

In most cases the proverbs are followed by a cultural/linguistic origin (e.g. Igbo, Jamaican, Haya). Where I have been unable to identify the precise origin of a proverb I have given a

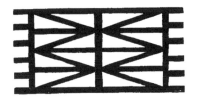

national or geographical provenance such as Caribbean, Ugandan, or African.

Readers will find some proverbs that they may think of as 'Western' in origin. For example "The love of money is the root of all evil" appears accredited to the Tshi people rather than Diogenes or St Paul. And while it may be tempting for Westerners to assume a Western origin, the universal nature of many proverbs makes their ownership debatable.

Conclusion

I have refrained from making any generalisations about the various cultural traditions I have come across in making this compilation. Bold statements about the character of proverbs or of a particular people require a degree of familiarity with the language, its cultural and historical setting, and the actual use of the proverbs that (with one exception) I cannot pretend to. Such an exercise, even when the prerequisites are met, is still liable to be little more than '...selecting evidence to persuade readers to accept an author's preconceived notions about the people in question.'[6] I hope readers will find as much to enjoy in this collection as I have.

PATRICK IBEKWE
London 1998

Footnotes

1 Though there are exceptions to this rule of anonymity, of which the best known in English are probably Shakespeare and Alexander Pope.

2 The writings of authors such as Cheikh Anta Diop have, since the mid-1970s, provided a useful counter to the practice of treating Ancient Egypt as part of a Mediterranean culture area by instead placing it firmly within the traditions of African Civilization. See his The *African Origin of Civilization*, 1974, Lawrence Hill & Co., Connecticut, and 'Precolonial Black Africa,' 1987, Lawrence Hill & Co.

3 Ambrose Adikamkwu Monye, *Proverbs In African Orature - The Aniocha-Igbo Experience*, University Press of America, Inc., Lanham, Maryland, 1996.

4 Richard Chevenix Trench, DD, Archbishop, *Proverbs And Their Lessons*, 10th Edition, London, Kegan Paul, Trench, Trubner & Co. Ltd, 1894.

5 Xavier Plissart, *Mamprussi Proverbs*, Musee Royal de l'Afrique Centrale, 1983.

6 Peter Isaac Seitel, *Proverbs And The Structure Of Metaphor Among The Haya Of Tanzania*, Facsimile Microfilm, University Microfilms International, Ann Arbor, Michigan, 1983.

Editor's note

In their English form, and perhaps as a result of translation, many of the proverbs were male in perspective and values. No doubt in some cases this is how the sayings evolved, reflecting roles and power relationships; and the use 'he' or 'a man' may have been taken to include women by those who originated, collected or translated the proverbs. However today this use of language is offensive to many people, men and women alike. With that in mind, many of the proverbs have been 'translated' once more to reflect a wider humanity.

A

Do not hurl a lance if you cannot control its aim – **ANCIENT EGYPTIAN**

Do not attempt what you cannot bring to a good end – **YORUBA**

All bïd [birds] can sing, but all bïd can't talk – **GUYANAN**

Don't ask the price if you don't have the money to buy – **MALAGASY**

A person who can't keep healthy cannot cure others – **UGANDAN**

One who does not get lost by night, will not get lost by day – **HAUSA**

The one who has a sharp knife is the one who eats the meat – **SWAHILI**

The one with the arrow is the one who shoots – **LAMBA**

She who is naturally gifted in anything becomes expert in it – **HAUSA**

He who knows how to go does not stumble – **SWAHILI**

If someone is about to give you a garment, look at the one on their own back – **HAUSA**

ABILITY

One carries the load one can – **TSHI**

A little man can fell a great oak – **HAITIAN**

A small axe fells a great tree – **MONGO**

A pilot who sees into the distance will not let the ship capsize – **ANCIENT EGYPTIAN**

A thing which cannot be lifted (i.e. accomplished) should never be undertaken – **YORUBA**

If we put a hammer in every person's hand, could they all become blacksmiths? – **AFRICAN**

Ole [old] fiddle play new tune – **JAMAICAN**

That which pecks on a rock should have a tough beak – **LUYIA**

The ability to dance is inherent in a lame person; it is the legs that are the handicap – **YORUBA**

The fowl eats yams, bites corn, [and yet] cries that she has no teeth – IGBO

The one who buys wine does not drink water – TSHI

The sound of the drum depends on the drummer – SHONA

You can' prevent bud from fly over you head, but you can prevent him mek nes' in you head
– JAMAICAN
You can't prevent the bird from flying over your head, but you can prevent him from making a nest in your head.

ABSENCE & PRESENCE

A little thing that is there is worth more than a big thing that has only been promised – GANDA

A master who is absent from his home loses his influence – GANDA

In the absence of moonlight the star shines – HAUSA

The meal of the latecomer is shared – OROMO

Those who are absent are always wrong – HAITIAN

When you are not there, your share is not there either – SWAHILI

Where there is no proper hen, a half-hen brags a lot – IGBO

ACCEPTANCE

Accept the weather as it comes and people as they are – HAITIAN

He who spoils what is his own has no quarrel – SWAHILI

If Death has come and killed your father and your mother, do not weep, saying, 'My father and my mother are dead,' but weep and say, 'I and my father and my mother will go with you.' – ASHANTI

Invite the gate-crasher first because he will never fail to come even when invited – OROMO

Man can't do bettah [better]; he say "No mattah." – GUYANAN

Recommendation is one thing, getting accepted is something else – HAITIAN

Those who work during the night should not blame the moon for disturbing them – YORUBA

What comes on your plate is what you swallow – UGANDAN

ACHIEVEMENT & SUCCESS

One who says 'It was too much for me,' does not try – GANDA

Running too fast does not guarantee that you reach your destination – SHONA

Slips outnumber falls – **KIKUYU**

The area covered by your life is not as important as what you build on it – **SWAHILI**

The child that will do well in life is not reared only on a good mat – **TSHI**

The end of the journey is reached by moving ahead – **OVAMBO**

The short person can become like the tall person, but the tall person has nothing else to excel in – **TSHI**

Aiming is not the same as hitting – **SWAHILI**

Those who have succeeded forget those who have helped them to succeed – **GANDA**

Trials [i.e. attempts] mean successes – **KIKUYU**

ACTION

Cross the bridge when you come to it – **SWAHILI**

Fe walk fe nuttin better dan fe si' down fe nuttin – **JAMAICAN**
To walk for nothing is better than to sit down for nothing

Glory does not come by calling – **KAMBA**

If the dog bites one's neighbour and no action is taken, it may bite one's child too – **YORUBA**

If words are silver, action is gold – **HAITIAN**

When the snake is in the house one need not discuss the matter at length – **EWE**

A person is in their deeds – **JABO**

A woman's deeds are her life – **IGBO**

All man can talk, but na [not] all can do – **GUYANAN**

Both good and evil deeds bring forth their own kinds – **EWE**

By his deeds we know a Man – **JABO**

Good word good, good deed bettah – **GUYANAN**

How is 'it won't be done' ever going to be done? – **MAMPRUSSI**

It is easier to know what to do than to do it – **SWAHILI**

It is one's deeds that are counted, not one's years – **AFRICAN**

When deeds speak, words are nothing – **AFRICAN**

ADAPTABILITY

If shade doesn't reach the crowned duiker [a small antelope], the crowned duiker will reach the shade – **MAMPRUSSI**
If the bag tears, then the shoulders get a rest – TSHI

If you carry water in a pot and it breaks on your head, you should just wash with water – **MAMPRUSSI**

It is possible for the owners of a house to warm themselves when their house is on fire – **KIKUYU**

The maggot in meat is itself meat – **HAUSA**

When thrown into the sea the stone said, 'After all, this is also a home.' – **UGANDAN**

ADVANTAGE

A thief knows the person from whom he steals; but the loser does not know (the thief) – **IGBO**

He who has refused relationship has given my fowl longer life. [i.e. it won't be killed to serve him food] – SHONA

In the land of the blind a one-eyed man is king – YORUBA

One-eye man a king a [of] blind country – JAMAICAN

The first to be at the well draws no muddy water – GIRIAMA

The place where a dog has fed it does not forget – SHONA

'Stop! let the quarrel come to an end': so says one whose friend is winning – GANDA

ADVICE

No instruction can have effect if there is dislike – ANCIENT EGYPTIAN

[The] fly that has nobody to caution it goes into the grave with the corpse – IGBO

A person who will not take advice gets knowledge when trouble overtakes him – XHOSA

Advice is like fire: it has to be obtained from others – SHONA

Advice is like mushrooms: you pick what you like – SHONA

An adviser does not advise himself – MAASAI

Conforming to good advice is better than sticking to one's own determinations – HAYA

Do not ask advice from the god and then pass by what he said – ANCIENT EGYPTIAN

Do not instruct someone who will not listen to you – ANCIENT EGYPTIAN

Even a fool may give a wise person counsel – SWAHILI

Even the clever one is advised – LUYIA

He that will not be counselled cannot be helped – UGANDAN

The one who advises you to buy a horse with a big belly will not help you feed it – HAITIAN

She who ignores advice does not resist when being prepared for burial – KIKUYU

He who is cutting a path doesn't see that it is crooked behind him – TSHI

People who are not warned may embark in a canoe made of earth – ITESO

A

The person who tells you to plough wants you to eat – SHONA

If someone says, 'Watch your conduct,' she has not insulted you – TSHI

If the vulture gives advice to the wolf, the wolf takes it – TSHI

If you are not told about it you go among people soiled – OVAMBO

One who refused advice was later seen bleeding – SHONA

Other people's wisdom prevents a chief from being called a fool – NIGERIAN

Stream said that it is because it has nobody to direct it that...it goes in a zig-zag way – IGBO

She who rebukes you puts you in good shape – EWE

AIMS & AMBITION

The person who pursues two rats will miss both – YORUBA

If you always work for someone else, you'll never get really big – HAITIAN

[A] man goes to market to get what he knows, not what he does not know – IGBO

It is to stand up that one changes from sitting – HAUSA

One time mistek [mistake], two time a [on] purpose – JAMAICAN

Where there is a purpose there is no failure – SWAHILI

Follow the river and find the sea – SWAHILI

Many ways to go but one way to come – BAJAN

You know where you are coming from, but not where you are going – MAASAI

If you hunt two partridges you will catch neither – CHAGGA

You cannot chase two gazelles – ZULU

She who seeks obtains – HAUSA

ANGER

A small pot boils quickly – SWAHILI

Anger breeds regret – MAMPRUSSI

Anger can make a person commit [deeds] which otherwise they would never do – TSHI

Anger is a warmth which lights itself – KRU

Anger is cured by silence – UGANDAN

Anger is like a stranger, it doesn't stay in only one person's house – TSHI

Anger is loss – SWAHILI

Anger is slavery – SWAHILI

Bad temper kills its owner – TWI

By getting angry, one shows that she is wrong – MALAGASY

If you are never angry, then you are unborn – BASA

In anger there is no intelligence – SUKUMA

The greatest remedy for anger is delay – SWAHILI

To remain quiet is the same as being angry – NUPE

5

Wrath does not build – TSONGA

It is better to spend the night in anger than in repentance – TAMASHEK

ANIMALS

A bird flies high above and its funeral is performed on the ground – MAMPRUSSI

A dog's tears drop inside – CHOPI

The hunter does not know how disappointed the dog is – GANDA

Train one for yourself; other people's dogs will not bark for you – OVAMBO

Wherever there are bones, there are dogs – MARTINIQUE

Crab had swum all sorts of water, but came to a woman's soup and could not swim again – IGBO

Dere is chance fe bud as well as fe gun – JAMAICAN
There is a chance for the bird as well as for the gun.

Even the greatest bird must come down from the sky to find a tree to roost upon – AFRICAN

For the elephant his tusks are not too heavy – PEDI

If you chase an animal and don't give it room to flee, it runs over you – TSHI

It is mysterious if a baboon falls from a tree – SHONA

Never follow a beast into its lair – TSWANA

The crocodile conceived and gave birth to trouble – HAUSA

The hyaena says that worldlings' saying and not doing leads to its laughing and crying – MAMPRUSSI

The squirrel can beat the rabbit climbing a tree, but then the rabbit makes the best stew and that sort of equalizes the thing – AFRICAN-AMERICAN

When a leopard catches a turtle, it turns it over and over in vain – TSHI

Whoever despises anything small has never trodden on a scorpion – HAUSA

You are afraid of a snake and it is afraid of you – OVAMBO

The ox is never weary of carrying his horns – HAITIAN

A dog that lets himself be tied deserves to be beaten – HAITIAN

Di stilles calf suck di mos' milk – CREOLE (BELIZE)
The stillest calf sucks the most milk.

Do not run after a hen with salt in your hand – THONGA

The tortoise breathes; it is the shell that conceals the fact – YORUBA

If you have caught the mother hen, you pick up her chicks without difficulty – TSHI

APPEARANCE

A child that is to be seen should not be shabby – IGBO

A leopard skin is attractive; inside it there is great anger – KAONDE

A red, fine-looking fig rots inwardly – ZULU

A silk dress doesn't mean (she has) clean under-garments – HAITIAN

A thing is worst on the day it is done – IGBO

A thing may resemble a tiger but it is not a tiger – IGBO

A turban does not make a man civilised – SWAHILI

All sweet na [isn't] sweet, all bittah na bittah – GUYANAN

As one's appearance, so they give seat – IGBO

Clothes are people – EWE

Clothes cober [cover] character – JAMAICAN

Deep silence conceals great noise – SWAHILI

Dog says that it is greeting the person who came to his house, but [his] harsh voice does not allow people to know – IGBO

Ebery howdee na howdee – GUYANAN
Every, 'how do you do,' isn't, 'how do you do.'

Having rainclouds is not the same as having rain – KIKUYU

However broken down is the spirit's shrine, the spirit is there all the same – JUKUN

If a madman takes away your cloth while you are at the water bathing, put on a cloth before pursuing him; for if you are naked people will think you are both mad – TSHI

It is in the quiet pool that the crocodiles live – SHONA

It is the still water that drowns a man – TSHI

Lilly [little] billy-goat hab [have] beard but big bull hab none – JAMAICAN

Making a fuss is not making haste – HAITIAN

Mice and rats: their fur is the same, but they do not do the same damage – MALAGASY

Mr 'Laugh in the eyes' - in his heart there are other things – NYANJA

No matter how beautiful a snake, it is dangerous – KAONDE

Not everything hot is fire – MAMPRUSSI

Orange yallah [yellow], but you na [don't] know if he sweet – GUYANAN

Saf'ly [softly] ribah [river] run deep – GUYANAN

Some people clean a tap an' dutty underneat' – JAMAICAN
Some people are clean on top and dirty underneath.

Still water has a deep bottom – SURINAMESE

A

The cloth is beautiful but its owner is ugly – EWE

The Nmampurusi say that resembling a chief is not a chief – MAMPRUSSI

The stone is wet, but not its inside – EWE

The teeth that laugh are also those that bite – HAUSA

To be smiled at is not to be loved – KIKUYU

White teeth don't indicate a good soul – SUKUMA

You see matty face, you no see he haat – GUYANAN
You see your friend's face but you don't see his heart.

What a splendid sugar cane! examine it, it is full of holes – MONGO

The one who looks nice does not complain (of the troubles of dressing and decoration) – KIKUYU

APPRECIATION

A one-eyed person does not thank god until he meets a blind person at prayer – NIGERIAN

A person is always thanked after death – TSWANA

A person is valued at death – IGBO

Bring me flowers while I am still alive – SWAHILI

Cow no know de wort'[h] a [of] her tail till she lose i'[t] – JAMAICAN

Gold should be sold to one who knows its value – YORUBA

The person to whom things are brought does not know the length of the road – OVAMBO

She who does not know an object cannot know its value – SWAHILI

He who does not know the advantage of light, let him enter darkness – SWAHILI

One who does not know you, does not value you – SWAHILI

He who is complete in all the members of his body cannot appreciate the value of that body – YORUBA

Instead of being rich at once it is better to be poor first – SWAHILI

One who has been pricked by a thorn values shoes – SWAHILI

People do not value that which costs them nothing – KIKUYU

Talk to a person who can understand and cook for a person who can be satisfied – LUVALE

The nose knows not the savour of salt – HAUSA

The rainbow might be better lookin' if 'twasn't such a cheap show – **AFRICAN-AMERICAN**

The usefulness of a well is known when it dries – **UGANDAN**

Those who wear pearls do not know how often the shark bites the leg of the diver – **AMHARIC**

Water is sweet when the weather is dry – **AFRICAN**

Whoever does not know you cannot appreciate you – **SWAHILI**

You have to suffer to appreciate the good times – **HAITIAN**

You will not see the importance of a well till the river runs dry – **TEMNE**

APPROPRIATENESS & SUITABILITY

A thing that comes fast must be pursued just as fast – **BEMBA**

A wound given in public is stitched [i.e. healed] in public – **KIKUYU**

Beckoning is the remedy for one who is afar – **HAUSA**

Cap no fit you, you no tek [take] i'[t] up – **JAMAICAN**

Dancing [to] the drum will be done where the drum is – **IGBO**

Do not send a wise man in a small matter when a big matter is waiting – **ANCIENT EGYPTIAN**

'Give me medicine at once!' doesn't make [allowance] for bad medicine – **TSHI**

Good partners don't find each other – **SHONA**

She who does not wrong is not done wrong – **SWAHILI**

In the daytime do we chase the black goat – **IGBO**

Nebber mek you sail too big fe you ship – **JAMAICAN**
Never make your sail too big for your ship.

One aims at a bird the way it flies – **YORUBA**

One doesn't climb a tree by the trunk and come down by the branches – **HAUSA**

One pulls [out] a thorn at the very place where it got in – **TSONGA**

Speak to the one who hears, send the one who is willing – **OROMO**

The joker isn't sent to call people to a death – **SUKUMA**

They do not climb the mountain running – **TSONGA**

What is not tough does not need a knife – **YORUBA**

What fits into the mouth, gives you a chance to chew it properly – **GANDA**

When the face of the drum is there, you don't beat the sides – **TSHI**

When the occasion comes, the proverb comes – **OJI**

When you mention a snake get hold of a stick – **SWAHILI**

AUTHORITY

A dog does not bark at its owner – **IGBO**

A king's servant is king – **IGBO**

The king's bodyguards are respected like the king – **IGBO**

Cat no deh, ratta tek over – **GUYANAN**
The cat's not there, the rat takes over.

Even if an okro plant is taller than a farmer she bends it to pick its fruits – **EWE**

Only the owner may say, 'Let's kill it.' – **UGANDAN**

The dog's owner is the one who can take the bone from its mouth – **JABO**

They let the dog alone because of the dog's owner – **MAMPRUSSI**

What is decided by legitimate authority is not resented by the subjects – **GANDA**

When a grown-up says something but doesn't do it, the children no longer fear him – **TSHI**

She who does not wrong is not done wrong — **SWAHILI**
In the daytime do we chase the black goat – **IGBO**

Nebber mek you sail too big fe you ship – **JAMAICAN**
Never make your sail too big for your ship.

One aims at a bird the way it flies – **YORUBA**

One doesn't climb a tree by the trunk and come down by the branches – **HAUSA**

One pulls [out] a thorn at the very place where it got in – **TSONGA**

Speak to the one who hears, send the one who is willing – **OROMO**

The joker isn't sent to call people to a death – **SUKUMA**

They do not climb the mountain running – **TSONGA**

What is not tough does not need a knife – **YORUBA**

What fits into the mouth, gives you a chance to chew it properly – **GANDA**

When the face of the drum is there, you don't beat the sides – **TSHI**

When the occasion comes, the proverb comes – **OJI**

When you mention a snake get hold of a stick – **SWAHILI**

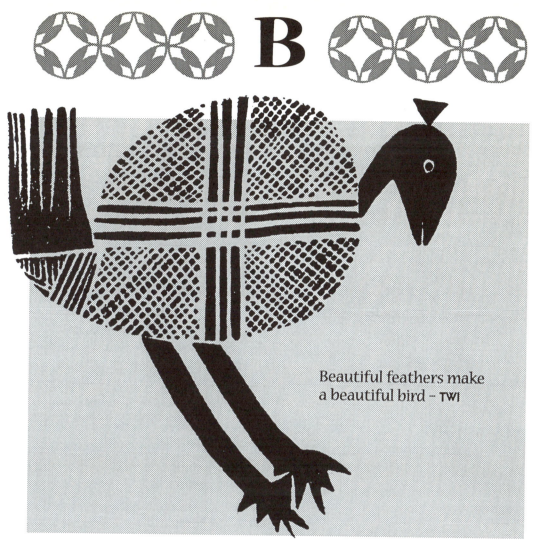

B

Beautiful feathers make
a beautiful bird – TWI

BEAUTY

A tree is beautiful when its trunk and its branches are beautiful – TSONGA

Beautiful 'ooman [woman], beautiful trouble – JAMAICAN

Beauty isn't wisdom – MAMPRUSSI

Beauty sells itself – UGANDAN

Beauty widout [without] grace like rose widout smell – JAMAICAN

She who marries beauty marries trouble – YORUBA

Many beautiful things are sour – HAITIAN

The beauty of the flower, but no fruit – SUKUMA

Verily, beauty is power – KANURI

BEGINNING

Good beginnings make good endings – SWAHILI

He that begins is not he that finishes – KIKUYU

If anyone is going to climb a tree she starts from the bottom, not from the top – TSHI

The beginning is always difficult – SWAHILI

The beginning is the most important part of the work – IGBO

Tortoise said that work that has been started is almost finished – IGBO

What has a beginning will have an end – IGBO

BEHAVIOUR

An adult who decides to behave like a child should be disciplined like a child – IGBO

A dog with a bone in his mouth does not bark – SHONA

Darg [dog] no howl if him hab [have] bone – JAMAICAN

Don't do it" is the best remedy for "let it not be known" – NUPE

Do what is right and neglect what is desired – FULANI

If a man jumps like a rat, a cat will catch him – IGBO

If the market isn't entered, leaving it is not difficult – MAMPRUSSI

If you are taking advantage of a fool, there is a wise woman there watching you – TSHI

If you behave well, you enjoy the benefits of your good character – TSHI

If you don't want a thing to get about don't do it – HAUSA

If you go to Pemba (island), you should put on a turban – SWAHILI

If you keep you finger-nail clean, you can put i'[t] in a gentleman['s] dish – JAMAICAN

If you want to stay in a place, watch your conduct – TSHI

It is better to refuse than to accept and not go – MALAGASY

It is not where you are but what you do there that matters – SWAHILI

Enquire about everything that you may understand it. Be good-tempered and magnanimous, that your disposition may be attractive – ANCIENT EGYPTIAN

Take not the gift of the strong man, nor repress the weak for him – ANCIENT EGYPTIAN

The guest who has broken the pot is not forgotten – KWELI

The person who is avoided by a woman is her loved one – YORUBA

When a (boy) child knows how to wash his hands well, he eats with the elders – TSHI

When a dog cannot bark it has a bone in its mouth – THONGA

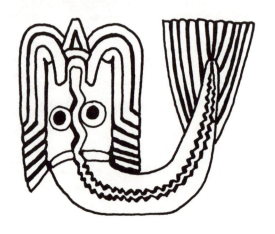

B

When two persons fight in the water, they both get wet – MALAGASY

When you go a-country weh [where] dem a-dance wid one foot, dance wid one foot too – GUYANAN

When you know that people are watching you, there are things that you don't do – HAITIAN

White attire attracts attention – SHONA

A person who is not disciplined cannot be cautioned – HAYA

An insolent child has only a mother (and no father) [i.e. is indulged but not disciplined] – GANDA

Over-discipline makes a child stunted – IGBO

If you know the behaviour of the cow you can catch her calf – OROMO

Gentleness in every kind of behaviour: that is the praise of the wise man – ANCIENT EGYPTIAN

BELATEDNESS

'Had I known,' comes too late – UGANDAN

He came after the cattle had already left the fold – TSWANA

He will separate the rams from the ewes when they have already mated – TSWANA

'If I come out of this alive I won't steal anymore.' – UGANDAN

'If uh [I] did know' does come too late – BAJAN

The tears of the rat come when it is caught in the trap – GANDA

When the animal is in the pot, it does not fear the knife – IDOMA

BETRAYAL & LOYALTY

He who betrayed you yesterday will not save you today – HAITIAN

He with whom you eat is the man who will kill you – SUKUMA

I do not mind the one who catches me, but she who gives me away – KIKUYU

If your friends don't betray you, your enemies won't catch you – HAITIAN

The antelope detests the one who announces its whereabouts more than the one who sees it [i.e. the hunter] – KIKUYU

If the cockroach chews on something, it blames the mouse – TSHI

No one roasts rotten meat and puts it in the mouth of their friend and then says, 'your mouth stinks.' – TSHI

One fears the person who sends one on an errand, not the person to whom one is sent – YORUBA

We must blame the thief first before we say that where the owner put her property [was] improper – YORUBA

When a clean person pollutes the air, people often blame the dirty person in their midst – LUYIA

Whether it was the tenant who seduced the landlord's wife, or the landlord who seduced the tenant's wife, it is the tenant who would leave the house – IGBO

The snake says it doesn't hate the person who kills it, but the one who calls out, 'Look at the snake!' – MARTINIQUE

Those who are nearest to you and know you, are the ones who betray you – HAITIAN

A servant serves a king, he serves the king well; a servant serves two kings, he is true to one – IGBO

You cannot serve two masters – HAYA

BOASTING & MODESTY

Boastin' man brudder a de liar – JAMAICAN
The boasting man is the brother of the liar.

Daag wah a-bark plenty a-run 'way time fo' bite – GUYANAN
The dog that barks plentifully runs away when it's time to bite.

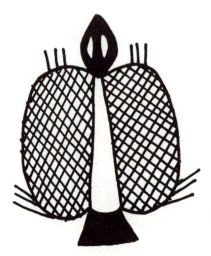

BLAME

A stinking black ant stinks because you pass where it is – KAONDE

All kind of fish nyam [eat] people, only shark get blame – JAMAICAN

Don't blame the ground you fall on, blame the obstacle that caused your fall – SWAHILI

The one that cannot dance says that the yard is stony – KIKUYU

Hollow gourd mek mos'[t] noise – **JAMAICAN**

One does not become great by claiming greatness – **XHOSA**

Rooster makes mo'[re] racket dan de hen w'at lay de aig [egg] – **AFRICAN-AMERICAN**

Some soldiers are only soldiers when talking – **KIKUYU**

That which runs alone claims to be a good runner – **LUYIA**

The one who asked for a knife wants it to be known that he has slaughtered a beast – **SHONA**

The one who wasn't there kills the buffalo – **UGANDAN**

When anyone says he will swallow an axe, hold the handle for him – **HAUSA**

'My mother is indeed the best baby carrier,' says the baby – **UGANDAN**

No put yourself in a barrel when match-box can hol'[d] you – **JAMAICAN**

The salt will not say of itself, 'I have a pleasant taste.' – **OJI**

BORROWING & LENDING

A debt does not settle another debt – **SHONA**

A debtor who borrows to pay their debt is still a debtor – **IGBO**

A loan is (almost) tantamount to a gift – **HAITIAN**

As always, the loaned pot got broken – **UGANDAN**

Better beg dan [than] borrow – **JAMAICAN**

Borrowed clothes do not fit the wearer – **SWAHILI**

'Borrowing is a wedding, paying back is mourning – **SWAHILI**

Borrowing is the first-born of poverty – **FULFULDE**

He who has only one suit can't lend it out – **HAITIAN**

It is better to lack something than to borrow – **SWAHILI**

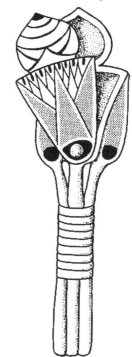

 **B**

Lending a friend money is to turn him into an enemy – SWAHILI

One cannot be in debt and still talk big – YORUBA

The [borrowed] ornament of another person tires the neck – KIKUYU

To borrow is sweet (easy); the day of payment is hard – HAUSA

To lend is to trust, to refuse to lend is to bury – SWAHILI

What is loaned to you can be taken back even when you still need it – LUYIA

While making a loan to somebody you might be in a sitting posture; but to request the loan back you will have to get up – GANDA

BUSINESS

A cat is not sold in a bag, but openly produced – GA

A gift is a gift, and a purchase is a purchase; so no one will thank you for saying "I sold it [to] you very cheap." – YORUBA

An article for sale has to be seen – SHONA

Bad things are sold cheaply – TSHI

In business there are no price waivers to one's parents and relatives – HAYA

In business, keep your eyes open – HAITIAN

One who bargains is shocked by the price – SWAHILI

The desire to cheat and the refusal to be cheated are the cause of the noise in the market – YORUBA

The smile on the seller's face is not the same when he comes to collect his money – HAITIAN

Trade does not quarrel. [i.e. sellers propitiate customers] – SWAHILI

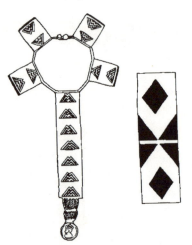

The chicken does not play near her eggs – **IGBO**

CARE & CAREFULNESS

A man knows the hut yet lights a torch to go inside – **MAMPRUSSI**

A person will observe you before she invites you – **LUYIA**

Being careful is not being a coward – **HAITIAN**

Count twice has defeated count once – **TSWANA**

Cut you[r] coat by you cloth, and mark twice befor' you cut once – **JAMAICAN**

Flies can't fall in[to] a tight-closed pot – **AFRICAN-AMERICAN**

Go round the long way, and arrive in safety – **GANDA**

He who selects coconuts with great care, gets an unripe one – **SWAHILI**

She who walks in the dark does not stumble – **SWAHILI**

If you attend to what is roasting, it will not be burnt – **YORUBA**

If you have not crossed the river, you should not abuse the crocodile – **IGBO**

It is better to take care beforehand than to ask pardon afterward – **LOUISIANA**

Look after the seedling for it to grow well – **KIKUYU**

Softly, softly ketch [catch] monkey – **JAMAICAN**

Tekin' [taking] time ent [isn't] laziness – **BAJAN**

The grasshopper that sleeps forgetfully wakes up in the mouth of the lizard – **IGBO**

The wound we took care of has healed – **OVAMBO**

Where the crocodile suns himself, you do not play – **KAONDE**

We don't build a nation with an 'I don't care' person – **TSHI**

Entering the water is not a 'bath' without scrubbing – **HAUSA**

Put down sof'ly nebber bruk plate – **JAMAICAN**
Put down softly never broke a plate.

CARELESSNESS

Carelessness in small things leads little by little to ruin – **GANDA**

He who has not chosen a place to sit down will get up with bits of straw on his garment – **FULFULDE**

Hen da cackle and da 'joyment himself, him no know say hawk da watch him – **JAMAICAN**
The hen that cackles and enjoys himself doesn't see the hawk that watches him.

Slackness turned all the tilled land back into bush – **KIKUYU**

When fowl merry, hawk ketch [catch] him chicken – **JAMAICAN**

Possessions without an account book are lost without noticing – **SWAHILI**

If you have no time to take care of your sickness, you get time to die – **TSHI**

The one who does a thing without finishing: it is as though they had never done it at all – **SWAHILI**

CAUSE & EFFECT

A good farm needs a good farmer – **HAITIAN**

[A] kind word has [a] good reply – **IGBO**

A bad sign (guide) brings you to a bad place – **SWAHILI**

A little worm may eat a big tree – **NAMIBIAN**

A person does not run among thorns for nothing. Either she is pursuing a snake or a snake is pursuing her – **YORUBA**

A person lays the bait tbefore they pull out a big fish – **MENDE**

A poor milker is known by its milking pail – **OVAMBO**

Big man no a-run fo' not'in' – **GUYANAN**
A big man doesn't run for nothing.

Chewing slowly is going to swallow – **KAMBA**

De [the] howlin' dog know what he sees – **AFRICAN-AMERICAN**

Fiah no deh, pat can't boil – **GUYANAN**
Fire not there, pot can't boil.

If a cow running up a hill is not pursuing something, then something is chasing her – **IGBO**

If nothing touches the palm leaves they do not rustle – **OJI**

If wick na [isn't] deh, lamp can't bu'n – **GUYANAN**

If you have chased a boy and he runs off, and you follow him, and when he is just about to enter the porch leading to his house, he comes back and stands waiting for you, he does not do that for nothing: his father is there – **HAUSA**

It is when the eye falls on the mat that [one] begins to feel sleepy – **JUKUN**

No sleep, no dream – **GA**

Smoke doesn't rise where there is no fire – **SHERBRO**

That which the ear hears the mouth replies to – **TSHI**

The hawk that is flying up in the air, its shadow will be seen on the ground – **IGBO**

The potter resembles his pot – **UGANDAN**

The prophet of hunger is not the cause of it – **UGANDAN**

There is no dust raised without a wind – **HAITIAN**

Throw away the bone and you will cease being troubled by flies – **HAUSA**

When breeze no blow, tree no shake – **JAMAICAN**

When the legs run away, the head must have seen the danger – **SHONA**

Where there is no wealth there is no poverty – **TSWANA**

CAUTION

A rider, like a monkey, never forgets that he might fall – **TSWANA**

'Careful' is a good way to go – **SWAHILI**

Do not push your finger in the mouth of a dog you did not bring up – **LUYIA**

Don't hurry to love someone. Perhaps she hates you. Don't hurry to hate her. Perhaps she loves you – FULFULDE

Fear the earth-worm if you are once bitten by a snake – EWE

General Coward and General Prudence are two different persons – HAITIAN

One who goes slowly (or carefully) goes far – UGANDAN

She who guards herself will not perish – OVAMBO

If something crawls at night, you shouldn't [try to] catch it – MAMPRUSSI

If the snake cares to live, it doesn't journey upon the high road – GUYANAN

If there are crocodiles in the water, take your bath in a gourd – HAUSA

If you call somebody else's dog, keep a stone in your hand – UGANDAN

Keep on the ground; wings expose you to danger – SHONA

Never throw away the old at the sight of the new – SHONA

Nobody measures the river with both of his feet – GA

One does not follow a snake into its hole – ZULU

One who is cautious kills the fearless – GANDA

Precaution does not mean cowardice – HAITIAN

Prudence is the mother of security – HAITIAN

Snake dat wan' fe [that wants to] grow up always stay in a him hole – JAMAICAN

Someone with a long tail doesn't cross [i.e. jump] over fire – MAMPRUSSI

The chicken says fear is life – EWE

The monkey says her eyes are his body's lookouts. – HAITIAN

The snake who does not hide does not last long – KURANKO

'Tone wall hab yeye – JAMAICAN
Stone wall has eye.

When snake bite you, you see lizard you run – JAMAICAN

When they sleep we should stay awake – SWAHILI

You always wade close to the banks of a river in which people have been drowned – EWE

CERTAINTY & UNCERTAINTY

Be pleased with what you have swallowed; that which is still in the cheek is for other people – **LOZI**

Count twice is better than to count once – **TSWANA**

Counting absent goats means counting even dead ones – **SHONA**

See de [the] candle light befo'[re] you blow out de match – **JAMAICAN**

The food that is in the mouth is not yet in the belly – **KIKUYU**

The white-tailed monkey says: 'what is in my cheeks is not mine, but what has gone into my belly is my own.' – **TSHI**

CHANGE

Ebery [every] day debil [devil] help tief, one day God help watchman – **JAMAICAN**

She who used to dance now looks on – **KIKUYU**

He who used to jump across now wades through – **KIKUYU**

If the music changes so does the dance – **HAUSA**

Night is followed by day, famine by abundance – **OVAMBO**

Out of crooked things develop straight things – **GANDA**

The rose petals fall, but the thorns remain – **HAITIAN**

What was yesterday's is not today's – **OVAMBO**

When a person is not as she used to be, she does not behave as she used to behave – **IGBO**

Where there was a storm, there is calm – **SWAHILI**

You cannot be too late to change – **SWAHILI**

You change your opinions for some biscuits – **HAITIAN**

What is bad we make good – **TWI**

CHARACTER

A full tin makes no noise, an empty one does – **TSONGA**

A good cock crows in any henhouse – **MARTINIQUE**

A good tree grows among thorns – **HAYA**

A leopard's cub is a leopard's cub, if it sees a wild beast it does not flee – **SHONA**

A man and his character - even rain cannot wash it off him – **HAUSA**

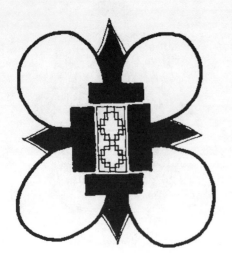

When rain beats on a leopard it wets it, but rain does not wash out its spots – ASHANTI

A parent bears the body, she does not bear the spirit – SWAHILI

A snake will shed its skin, its poison never – NAMIBIAN

A spotted cow gives birth to a spotted calf – LUYIA

A white fowl is still white, even though you may dip it in palm oil – TEMNE

An empty bag cannot stand – TEMNE

Bag no full, he can't 'tan' up – GUYANAN
If the bag isn't full it can't stand up.

As soon as the monkey has climbed a tree, it will start abusing you from its elevated position – NAMIBIAN

Before you buy a kid you must know the mother – EWE

Character is a god; according to the way you behave it supports you – YORUBA

Character is a line on a rock – FULANI

Driving away by means of character is better than driving away with a stick – HAUSA

Flies are attracted to a smelling thing – LAMBA

From a donkey you always expect a kick – OVAMBO

Have a crooked neck but not crooked morals – SUKUMA

She who gave to me is the same as she who withheld from you – SWAHILI

He who ridicules a deformed person becomes deformed himself – SWAHILI

If someone hates you, don't let her find you hateful – TSHI

If you're worthless in the province, you're also worthless in the Capital – HAITIAN

In order to chase a dog away throw it a bone – SHONA

Iron is passed through fire to be hardened – SWAHILI

Li'l [little] Judas and big Judas all one price – BAJAN

Nobleness is not noble ancestry – SWAHILI

One does not discover the heart of a brother if one has not begged from him in want – ANCIENT EGYPTIAN

Rain doesn't kill the strength of hot pepper – HAITIAN

The calabash that has a bottom is the one that stands most securely – KAMBA

The cat does not watch over fried fish – EWE

The crocodile conceived and brought forth trouble – HAUSA

The hyena doesn't guard the corpse – FIPA

The pup of a leopard claws like its mother – KIKUYU

The stump that stays in a river for a hundred years does not become a crocodile – EWE

The tree fell the way it leant – FIPA

Though the rain beats on a stone, the stone remains where it is – TSHI

What one hyena does, all hyenas will do – NAMIBIAN

What the dog barks at is the same as what the sheep looks meekly at – YORUBA

You can find a person who gives another a hen to take care of for him, and he counts the eggs the hen lays [while in the custody of the other] ; and you can find a person who presents another with a horse together with the saddle – YORUBA

You nebber see full bag ben'[d] – JAMAICAN

You talk wid [with] hog you can'[t] expect nuttin' but grunt – JAMAICAN

A de [it's the] quiet cow de butcher kill – JAMAICAN

A timid person does not enjoy the world – NUPE

Empty not your soul to everybody and do not diminish thereby your importance – ANCIENT EGYPTIAN

He who is quiet about his affairs will find them taken no notice of – YORUBA

If you are shy of someone, it is [as if] you fear him – TSHI

The polite and shy old lady let people bury her alive – UGANDAN

The shy stay hungry – UGANDAN

Empty barrels make the most noise – HAITIAN

The drum makes a great fuss because it is empty inside – TRINIDADIAN

Wagon makes the loudest noise when it's goin'[g] out empty – AFRICAN-AMERICAN

CHILDREN

[A] child is greater than money – IGBO

[At] whatever age a child gets a problem, at the same age she has to shoulder the responsibility [of solving it] – IGBO

A captive who was exchanged [for] his son is not yet free – IGBO

A child grows up as she is brought up – SWAHILI

A child is an axe: when it cuts you, you still pick it up and put it on your shoulder – BEMBA

A child normally follows the ways of the parents – HAYA

A child sees within her limits – IGBO

A child should be disciplined before it is too late – HAYA

A child that asks questions isn't stupid – EWE

A child that cries always at nothing, no one knows when he is really harmed – IGBO

A child thinks 'They'll beat me,' and not, 'This will shame me.' – UGANDAN

A child's good manners give great credit to the parents – SWAHILI

A tree is straightened when it is young – OVAMBO

Absence does not raise a child – TSHI

An orphan advises himself/herself – SHONA

An ugly child of your own is more to you than a beautiful one belonging to your neighbour – GANDA

Bend the stick while it is still green – MAMPRUSSI

Chick, find food [for] your mother; she used to search for it for you – OVAMBO

Children are more than wealth – UGANDAN

Children are not a cause for rejoicing in themselves; it is the man who is buried by his children that has had children – YORUBA

Children are the wealth and happiness of the poor – HAITIAN

Children never have enough when they cater for themselves – GANDA

Children suck dem mudda when dem young, dem fada when dem ole – JAMAICAN
Children suck their mother when they are young, their father when they are old [drain them of money].

Do not remember the child when you have already swallowed the food – SHONA

Even if you do not want to give [the] mother, you still give [to] her because of the child – IGBO

She who leaves a child lives eternally – CHAGGA

If a child tells me where he is going, I will tell him what to say – IGBO

If you love other people's children, you will love your own even more – SWAHILI

It is easy to climb but descending will cause one to call for his mother – SHONA

C

Little palm tree, stop crying, your child is the tall palm tree - TSHI

Many children, many graves - TSONGA

No one sends a child on a difficult errand and gets angry if she does not perform it well - ASHANTI

Sen' out pickney, you' foot res', but you' heart no res' - JAMAICAN
Send a child and your foot rests but your heart doesn't rest.

Sometin' 'pwoil a marnin nebber tun good a night - JAMAICAN
Something spoiled in the morning never turns good at night..

The child buys what she likes - TSHI

The infant makes laws - TSONGA

The man who has children should refrain from taking too many risks - HAITIAN

The monkey never finds her child ugly - HAITIAN

The woman whose sons have died is richer than a barren woman - KIKUYU

There is no wealth where there are no children - JABO

To be a child is painful - TSHI

To bear children is wealth, to dress oneself is nothing but colour - TSONGA

To bear many children means to shed plenty of tears - SHONA

To send a small child means to send oneself - SHONA

To tell a child you need to explain yourself thoroughly - SHONA

To walk with a little child is to wait for him - KAONDE

What the child says, she has heard it at home - WOLOF

Whatever the parents talk at midnight, the children talk at midday - OROMO

When a child does what she is not supposed to do, she suffers what she is not supposed to suffer - TSHI

When the mother goat breaks into the yam store her kid watches her - IGBO

When you have no mother and you go to someone's house to play and the mother is advising her children, you take her advice for yourself - TSHI

Where the mother sends (her children), the childless goes himself - GANDA

C

Who leaves a child behind keeps looking back – FIPA

With the right hand they thrash a child, and with the left draw it to them – NUPE

You make donkeys out of other people's children; out of your own you make horses that do not carry sticks – OVAMBO

Young bud [bird] no fly too fur [far] – JAMAICAN

The child who does not listen to his father never grows old – ITESO

A child that repeats the proverbs of his father - let him repay the debts of his father – IGBO

If a child always likes to be with the elders, she will grow up too fast – TSHI

CHOICE & OPTIONS

A person becomes what she wants to become – SWAHILI

A thorn with which one has pricked one's self of one's own accord does not pain – NYIKA

If one comes to a fork of the road in a strange country, she stops to think – JABO

If the river prevent crossing it will not prevent turning back – HAUSA

If you have decided to eat a dog, eat a fat one – UGANDAN

If you sleep under a tree, you can't prevent the leaf from falling on you – HAITIAN

Once you make up your mind to cross a river by walking through, you do not complain of getting your stomach wet – EWE

One who chooses is never without desire – SWAHILI

One's own chosen meat is without a] bone. [i.e. is faultless] – KIKUYU

The beads one has chosen have no imperfection – KIKUYU

The load you bind for yourself is not heavy – SWAHILI

The mouth takes what the eyes approve – IGBO

To go does not prevent a person from returning – KIKUYU

When a woman goes to dance she will choose that person who is better than her husband – IGBO

When it is impossible to cross a river, it will not be impossible to go back – IGBO

The work which one has imposed on oneself is never too much – **KIKUYU**

Don' heng all yuh clothes 'pon one nail – **BAJAN**
Don't hang all your clothes upon one nail.

The pigeon with only one source of food is likely to die of hunger – **KIKUYU**

CLEVERNESS

One who knows everything at times draws water with a basket – **IGBO**

A person does not become clever by carrying books along – **SWAHILI**

An intelligent child needs but one lesson – **MONGO**

An intelligent person does not have to have everything spelt out for her – **KIKUYU**

Occasionally, a man with right smart education can't find his knife when it gets in the wrong pocket – **AFRICAN-AMERICAN**

˙One who explains things to an intelligent person need not tire herself out talking – **GANDA**

Somebody's wit is also his folly – **SWAHILI**

To point out is enough for a sensible person – **HAUSA**

What cleverness hides, cleverness will reveal – **FULANI**

Where a clever doctor fails, try one less clever – **TSWANA**

Wits are wealth – **SWAHILI**

CO-OPERATION

An elephant dies because of many spears – **LUVALE**

If everyone helps to hold up the sky, then one person does not become tired – **TSHI**

If two [people] carry a log, it doesn't press hard on their heads – **TSHI**

Many hands catch even a strong person – **TSHI**

One fierce person can't overcome two frail ones – **FIPA**

One finger can'[t] ketch [catch] louse – **JAMAICAN**

One finger does not lift a heavy load – **TWI**

One hand must wash the other – **TSWANA**

One leg cannot dance alone – **THONGA**

COMMONSENSE

A goat will never go into the bush to seek a hyena – ANGASS

An egg does not fight a rock – MALAGASY

Betta short a pence dan short a sense – JAMAICAN

Common sense better dan [than] education – CREOLE (BELIZE)

Common sense born before book – BAJAN

Do not inhabit it [a dwelling place] before you have inspected it – MAASAI

Don't measure poles in the forest. – UGANDAN
Rather bring them home as they are and cut them to size when actually building the hut

Don't shoot an arrow in the dark – SWAHILI

Don't throw stones where you keep bottles – TEMNE

One who sees the tortoise in tears needn't ask it if all is well – IGBO

He who steals a zana mat finds it too much to hide up his sleeve – HAUSA

One who takes a light to find the whereabouts of a snake should commence at his feet – GOGO

Hen 'gree fe hatch duck egg, but him no 'gree fe tek duck-pickney fe swim – JAMAICAN
The hen agrees to hatch the duck's egg, but not to take the duckling for a swim.

I do not sow ground-nuts when the monkey is watching – TIV

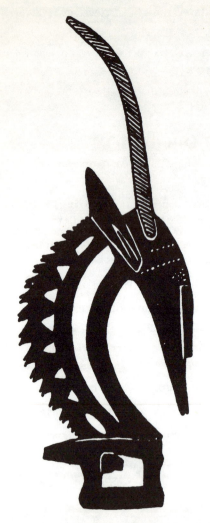

One man beat de bush and de oder ketch de bud – JAMAICAN

The attempt exceeds the ability of one, not of a multitude – EFIK

The hand of the child cannot reach the shelf, nor [can] the hand of the adult get through the neck of the gourd – YORUBA

What is looked for by many will have a finder – GANDA

When the right hand washes the left, the left should also wash the right – IGBO

If the head is in the market and the cap is in the market, no one takes the cap home to try it on – IDOMA

If you are on the river-side, you don't spit saliva to wash your hands – MAMPRUSSI

Look for the black goat while it is day – IGBO

Man wid sense na go shub he head a-hole – GUYANAN
A man with sense doesn't go and shove his head inside a hole.

Never give up what you have seen for what you have heard – SWAHILI

No heng you hat higher dan you can reach – CREOLE (BELIZE)
Don't hang your hat higher than you can reach.

No one hides himself and then lights a fire – TSHI

Nobody makes a bargain to take the burden and pay the debts – EWE

Nobody takes a dead person's amulet and says to it: 'Give me life and health!' – ANCIENT EGYPTIAN

Sharpen knife, lef' place fe han' hol' – JAMAICAN
In sharpening a knife, leave a place for the hand-hold.

Start looking for your cloth where you took your bath – IGBO

The man whose skill in throwing a spear is known: you don't wait till he brandishes it at you – GANDA

'There are forty kinds of lunacy, but only one kind of commonsense – SOUTHERN AFRICA

When the bait is more than the fish 'tis time to stop fishing – AFRICAN-AMERICAN

Where there are chickens don't spill millet – SWAHILI

You don't ask for the food-box of someone who died of starvation – TSHI

You don't cut its branches while perching on the tree – MAMPRUSSI

You don't run for water that's far away – SUKUMA

You estimate the size of an animal before you hit it with a stick – TSHI

You have no sense left: like the man who quarrels where he works for food; will [he] not go there again tomorrow? – GANDA

You haven't crossed the river yet; don't curse at the crocodile's mother – TRINIDADIAN

You see somebody on top of the palm-tree and ask whether he is healthy or not; if he is not in good health, could he have climbed the palm-tree? – YORUBA

You'll see that the man who grinds poison of the Ng'hale tree never licks his fingers – SUKUMA

What you have lost at sea, look for it on the beach – SWAHILI

COMPANIONS

A bad cowry-shell looks quite respectable in a string of [a] hundred – GANDA

A person is judged in accordance with the company she keeps – YORUBA

A person who lives with thieves, what can he produce but theft? – SWAHILI

Don't be like the shadow: a constant companion, but not a comrade – MALAGASY

Go with a poisoner and you will poison – SUKUMA

Heaps of good cotton stalks get chopped up from association with the weeds – AFRICAN-AMERICAN

If pigeon fly wid blackbird 'e gine get shot – BAJAN
If the pigeon flies with the blackbird he's going to get shot.

If the crab is small it associates with a smaller kind of crab – NYANG

If you associate with a fool, you also become a fool – TWI

If you go with donkeys, you're going to carry a load – HAITIAN

It is better to be alone than to have bad company – OROMO

One dirty finger dirties those remaining – MAMPRUSSI

Tell me your friend and I shall tell you your character – SWAHILI

The friend of a thief is a thief – NUPE

The horse which grazes with a donkey kicks like the donkeys – OROMO

To stay together is not the same as to have the same type of life – KIKUYU

When you sleep wid darg [dog] you ketch [catch] him flea – JAMAICAN

COMPARISON

[It is] for the table and not for sale [that] a chicken excels a horse – HAUSA

A little is bettah dan [than] not'[h]in'[g] – GUYANAN

Better than having no husband is to be married to a deaf one – GANDA

If gold rus'[ts], wha'[t] will iron do? – **BAJAN**

Rags are better than nakedness – **HAITI**

The frog does not have as much knowledge of the river as the fish – **YORUBA**

The tree which has been too much for the baboon, the monkey cannot climb – **SWAHILI**

When the moon is not full, the stars are bright – **HAUSA**

COMPLACENCY & OVERCONFIDENCE

A sharp knife can become blunt – **KIKUYU**

To be praised is to be ruined – **KIKUYU**

When darg da trot, him no know wha' da follow him – **JAMAICAN**
When the dog trots (i.e. strolls) he doesn't know what follows him.

'Easy' does not always happen – **SWAHILI**

'I know it perfectly' prevents the wasp from learning to make honey – **YORUBA**

A bathing place you are familiar with brings forth a crocodile bite – **TONGA**

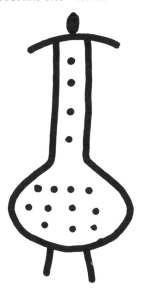

It is on the path you do not fear that the wild beast catches you – **TSHI**

Just because it's near doesn't necessarily mean that you'll get there – **HAITIAN**

The bocor (medicine man) gives you a protective charm, but he doesn't tell you to sleep in the middle of the highway – **HAITI**

The expert swimmer is carried away by the water – **ZULU**

The food in the mouth is not in the stomach – **KIKUYU**

The grass which you call contemptible may one day pierce your eye – **ANGASS**

CONFIDENCE

[A] child stands by the way and abuses passers by: he trusts that his father is near – **IGBO**

A dog swallowing a bone is confident of its power to break it – **SHONA**

One who challenges you to fight is confident of winning – **UGANDAN**

She who goes into a river may fear, but the river does not fear – **YORUBA**

If the monkey laughs he knows that his stronghold is nearby – SWAHILI

CONSEQUENCES

The mouth which ate pepper is the one which pepper affected – IDOMA

As they prepare the bed for you so you will sleep – SWAHILI

Being caught is not being imprisoned – KIKUYU

Crooked stick, crooked shadder [shadow] – JAMAICAN

Do not show caterpillars leaves – MONGO

One who asks questions cannot avoid the answers – IGBO

The person who despises one leader doesn't despise just one person – UGANDAN

One who fishes on land will catch only lizards – MALAGASY

He who provokes a war must be sure that he knows how to fight – TSONGA

One who rejects a call, rejects what she is called for – SWAHILI

He who stirs up a wasps' nest must be sure that he is able to run – TSONGA

If it rots it will stink – MAMPRUSSI

If one's relative is eating poisonous insects and one does not warn her, the horrible pain in the night [that she suffers] will make one sleepless – YORUBA

One who is in a position of authority never coughs – MONGO

He who swallows a fruit stone has a high opinion of (or trusts) his throat – TSONGA

If you hear a blind man saying, 'I can beat you,' it implies that he has some support – SHONA

The bird that pecks at a rock trusts in the strength of its beak – UGANDAN

The ground squirrel runs slowly because it trusts its hole which is nearby – ACHOLI

When the mouse laughs at the cat, there is a hole – WOLOF

C

If the men are not slain, the women are not carried off – ASHANTI

If the one running after [a person] does not stop, the one pursued should not stop – TEMNE

If they are praising your climbing skill, they are also predicting your fall – EWE

If we blind the eyes in order not to see a wicked person, how shall we be able to see a good person? – XHOSA

If you accept to be tied, you accept to be pulled – MAMPRUSSI

If you are unkind and get involved in a fight, you won't get many supporters – TSHI

If you burn a house you can't hide the smoke – UGANDAN

If you burn the savannah do not get angry at the black ashes – UGANDAN

If you destroy a bridge, be sure you can swim – SWAHILI

If you do what you shouldn't do, you will see what you shouldn't see – TSHI

If you eat a candle, you'll excrete a wick – HAITIAN

If you pass faeces on the road, you step on it [returning] – MAMPRUSSI

If yuh [you] sell all yuh got yuh mus'[t] buy all yuh want – BAJAN

It is easy enough to steal a fowl but where are you going to eat it? – HAUSA

It is not good to defeat a rich person – IGBO

Leopard carries off someone, it carries his shadow [too] – IGBO

Many births mean many burials – KIKUYU

She who has undressed shouldn't fear a long penis – UGANDAN

The limit of a sore is the limit to which the matter from the sore spreads – HAUSA

The one who skins a pole-cat should not resent its stench – SHONA

The urine passed into the river comes back to us as drinking water – IGBO

Those who sent the thief to go and steal also sent the farmer after him – YORUBA

Water poured on the head will reach the feet – OROMO

What is sown will sprout – OROMO

C

Whatever [a person] does will one day affect her – IGBO

When a box is carried, what is inside the box is also carried – TSHI

When a child does what a grown-up does, she suffers what a grown-up suffers – TSHI

When a child is learning how to climb, the mother will be learning how to cry – IGBO

When the eldest son is too fat, the youngest is too thin – MALAGASY

Where a hammer beats repeatedly, there will be a crack – GANDA

Where the penis enters, there the child comes out – MAMPRUSSI

Where two elephants engage in a fight, the grass there will never fight [i.e. flourish] again – YORUBA

If you can' mek i' better, you hab fe leave i' so – JAMAICAN
If you can't make it better, you have to leave it so [i.e. as it is].

A child in the mother's womb unfailingly takes some qualities from her – GANDA

Anything born [of a] snake must be very long – IGBO

The son of the zebra also has stripes – SUKUMA

CONSIDERATION

'Hold my baby like you hold yours,' said the woman – OROMO

A heart that does not consider a word carefully, makes you speak something your neighbour won't forget – GANDA

A heart that does not reflect will speak a thoughtless word – GANDA

At night one ponders about the matter, in the morning it is understood in another way – OVAMBO

Chew until it is soft before you swallow – LUYIA

Do not say the first thing that comes into your head – NANDI

Fowl tread [u]pon him chicken, but him no tread too hard – JAMAICAN

He who has no manners does not care about others – SWAHILI

One who spoils (or disarranges) anything should know how to re-arrange it – TEMNE

It is better to sleep on what you intend doing than to stay awake over what you have done – IGBO

The thought to commit a suicide was not in one day – IGBO

She who thinks of you in sickness will think of you in death – KONGO

If the heart worries there is no lack of tears – OROMO

She who advises you to run away from danger is on your side – LUYIA

One who uses a big bundle of firewood for cooking, has no consideration for one who has to gather the firewood – GANDA

Pound worth of fret never pay quarter worth of debt – CARIBBEAN

To send someone rests the feet, but not the heart – KANURI

CONSULTATION

Tortoise says: one person alone has no wisdom – JABO

A person who habitually says 'I do not ask others,' is not wise (or: knows little) – GANDA

As your neighbour speaks so you reason – AFRICAN

Many heads, much knowledge – EWE

One head does not go a-counselling – GA

One head does not consume all knowledge – MAASAI

One who asks the way cannot get lost – SWAHILI

One who does not tell you where she is going, cannot be looked for – GANDA

COURAGE & DARING

Courage is not the same as fighting someone stronger than you – SWAHILI

If a ram is brave, its courage comes from its heart: its courage is from its heart not from its horns; its courage is from its heart and not from its head – TSHI

If you like honey, fear not the bees – WOLOF

It's easy to be daring if you are well-guarded – SHONA

Sometimes you need more courage to retreat than to advance – HAITIAN

Strength does not correspond with courage – KIKUYU

True courage is knowing how to suffer – HAITIAN

We risk death and find safety – JABO

What is left by the trembling one is taken by the one who climbs the tree – OVAMBO

If you apologize before saying something bad, it will not be taken badly – TSHI

If you go to rat's village and it is eating palm nuts, you eat some too – TSHI

It is a mere formality for a small bird to invite an elephant in to its nest – SHONA

One who often says to you, 'thank you,' finishes off your things – GANDA

Pleasant words or politeness will tame the most cruel – HAYA

Politeness costs so little and is worth so much – HAITIAN

Politeness is gold – SWAHILI

To salute a dwarf by bowing will not prevent you from rising to your full height again – HAUSA

When you go to someone else's house and the owner is squatting there on the ground, you do not ask for a stool – ASHANTI

To dance as the drum beats – HAITIAN

Where flies are eaten, eat them – UGANDAN

COWARDICE

A cowardly hyena lives longer – TONGA

Coward keep whole bone – GUYANAN

Coward, strangle your fear, or else you will strangle yourself – OVAMBO

COURTESY

'Howdee' an' 'tenkee' break no bones – GUYANAN

'How do you do,' and 'thank you' break no bones.

He who goes to another's house leaves his bad habits at the door – RWANDA

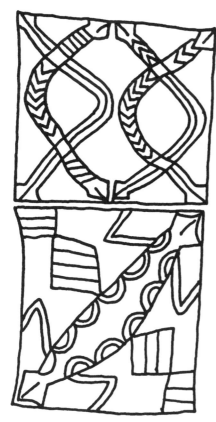

A sick fowl is never sold near home – IGBO

Cunning better dan [than] strong – BAHAMIAN

Do not call a dog while you are holding a stick – TSONGA

Ebery [every] shut eye na [not] a-sleep – GUYANAN

One who walks stealthily is found by the one who is hiding furtively – EWE

If you are too smart to pay the doctor, you had better be too smart to get sick – TSWANA

If you sell a drum in your own village, you get the money and keep the sound – MALAGASY

Good manners is cowardice – OVAMBO

In the house of the coward there is no weeping – PEDI

Only courageous at home – IGBO

Reasoning is the shackle of the coward – TAMASHEK

The coward's flight runs aimlessly – MAMPRUSSI

In the house of the cowards, there are no cries of mourning – TSONGA

CRAFTINESS

A cunning man likes the company of a fool – KIKUYU

A lion who goes quietly is the one who eats meat – SWAHILI

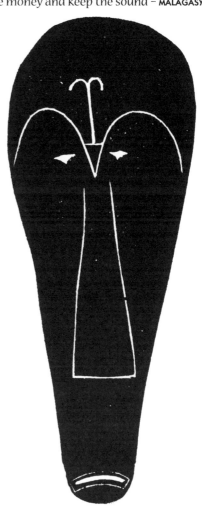

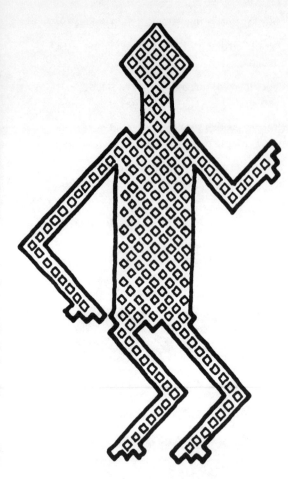

CRITICISM

Criticism of the brave is behind his back –
IGBO

Do not belittle what you did not cultivate –
UGANDAN

Do not criticize others while you are not
yourself perfect – **HAYA**

Finger nebber [never] say, 'Look yere [here],'
him say, 'Look yander [yonder].' – **JAMAICAN**

If you do not accept criticism you must look
after yourself alone – **TSONGA**

Only the speech is criticized, not the woman
herself – **SOUTHERN AFRICA**

Rebuke reflects behaviour – **UGANDAN**

The memory of a reprimand is like the wind:
it can be felt but not heard – **MALAGASY**

Whoever objects to the moon's position, let
them climb up and adjust it – **HAUSA**

Play wid de chil' fe de good a de nurse.[i.e. it is
the woman you are really interested in] –
JAMAICAN
Play with the child for the good of the nurse.

The little 'kasanke' (small red finch)
encourages the fighting cocks (in order to get
feathers for its nest) – **GANDA**

To a relative give a mixture of grain and chaff
(to convince him that your stock is limited) –
LUYIA

Too much sharpness cuts the sharpener –
KIKUYU

D

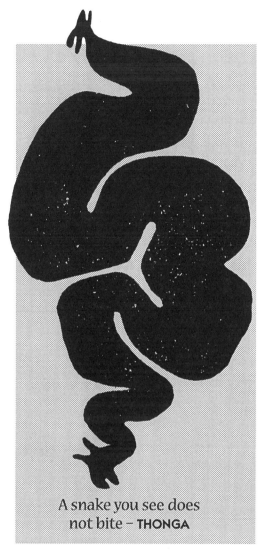

A snake you see does not bite – THONGA

DANGER & RISK

A danger escaped is no guarantee for the future – KIKUYU

A quiet lion is one that finishes people – GIRIAMA

A snake bites where it reaches – SWAHILI

Danger doesn't return where it's already known – FIPA

Danger makes a person rise from bed – KIKUYU

Do not lay hold of a man who has drawn a knife – YORUBA

Even a deadly mushroom tastes nice – GANDA

Fear surrounds the place where a snake disappeared into the bush – JABO

If you get you han' in a debil mout', tek time tek i' out – JAMAICAN
If you get your hand inside the devil's mouth, take time in removing it.

Man han'[d] in a lion mout'[h] him mus tek [take] time draw i'[t] out – JAMAICAN

No mine [never mind] how cockroach drunk, him no walk pas'[t] fowl-yard – JAMAICAN

One doesn't follow a wild beast into its lair – LAMBA

One gets drowned even in shallow water – ZULU

Sof'[t]ly riber [river] run deep – JAMAICAN

Staying and staring is the death of the buck – OVAMBO

Sun set but danger nebber [never] set – JAMAICAN

That which is deadly does not lack [a] sweet scent – UGANDAN

The butterfly that brushes against thorns will tear its wings – YORUBA

The lightening that kills doesn't thunder – UGANDAN

The meal you love most, that's what's going to choke you – HAITIAN

The rat knows full well that, if the cat is old and feeble, its claws are not – HAITIAN

The snake that bit itself won't spare a passer-by – UGANDAN

The tortoise says 'The hero should not be ashamed of fleeing from danger.' – TWI

To take a risk: as when an epileptic goes to war – GANDA

Water can drown the ferryman, much more the learner – HAUSA

When rat see cat, [h]e nebbah [never] laugh – GUYANAN

When two deer are fighting and they see a lion, they run off together – TSHI

DEATH

At someone's funeral we weep for our own mothers and fathers – TSHI

Beauty and pride go to the grave – SWAHILI

Death comes but once – EFIK

Death does not know the leader – IGBO

Death don't see no difference [be]'tween the big house and the cabin – AFRICAN-AMERICAN

Death is in the leg: we walk with it – THONGA

Death is like a spoilt child: it gets everything – NAMIBIAN

Death is the greatest physician that cures all diseases – IGBO

Death never makes appointments with people – KIKUYU

Even the proud one will be covered with earth – OVAMBO

Even the richest have only one shroud – HAITIAN

Every kind of death is the same – TSHI

Fear is no obstacle to death – BAMBARA

God created death but death killed Him – TSHI

I am not dead yet. I can suffer a bit more – NAMIBIAN

If death has come and not yet gone away, you don't tell it: 'I'm still here.' – TSHI

It is better to die some other day than dying today – SWAHILI

It is death that can make an antelope enter into a house in town – YORUBA

It is death which is feared, and it is also death which is inevitable – OROMO

It's when death comes that you think about your life – **MAURITIAN**

Just at the moment I am bad, (but) when I die you will remember me – **SWAHILI**

Many days are overcome by one death – **SUKUMA**

No one knows the messenger of death – **SHERBRO**

People's plans do not always succeed but death's plans do – **TSWANA**

Poverty may be invited but death comes on its own – **SHONA**

Prayers and tears don't stop you from dying – **HAITIAN**

Strength does not prevent one from dying – **KIKUYU**

The burial ceremonies are quite bothersome when the dead calls for more attention than when he was alive – **HAYA**

The days being finished, there is no medicine – **KANURI / BORNU**

The dead goat is not afraid of the hunter's gun – **EWE**

[The] death of your beloved reminds you of your turn – **HAYA**

The duiker [antelope] does not go to market, but its skin does – **ASHANTI**

The experience of the last person to die will be unimagineable – **YORUBA**

The hoe of death does not weed in only one place – **TSHI**

When the messenger of death cometh to carry thee away, let him find thee prepared – **ANCIENT EGYPTIAN**

The river gives no compensation, earth receives no ransom – **MONGO**

The thirst of death is not quenched – **KIKUYU**

There is no beginning that has no end – **SWAHILI**

Those who die through ignorance are many; those who die because they are intelligent are few – **YORUBA**

Though you give to it, it will not be satisfied – **OVAMBO**

What you love, death also loves – **TWI**

When death kills your contemporary, it is a warning to yourself – **YORUBA**

When one is dead, is then everything dead? – **NYANG**

The mouse says 'He who kills me does not hurt me as much as he who throws me on the ground after I am dead.' – TSHI

The death of the suicide cannot be avenged – EWE

The thoughts after which a man killed himself [were] not deliberated upon only over one night, but many nights – IGBO

DESIRE

One who eats what she has, her desire is for what she has not – IGBO

A toothless person yearns for meat – OROMO

Desires tie – KIKUYU

If plain water was satisfying enough, then the fish would not take the hook – TSHI

If you want to be warm, go near the fire – NAMIBIAN

The eyes of those who will eat and of those who will not eat are all looking at the cow being slaughtered – GANDA

What the eye has seen is what the hand goes after – EWE

What the eyes do not see, the heart doesn't desire – HAITIAN

What you yearn for makes you throw away what you have – UGANDAN

Where the heart longs to be the path never reaches – SHONA

You believe easily what you want to believe – HAITIAN

When one's contemporaries begin to die, one [should] have the forefeeling of death – YORUBA

You shouldn't become thin by always thinking of the day when you will die – TSHI

Yuh dead longer dan yuh live – BAJAN
You're dead longer than you're alive.

A creature is not completely created until death – SWAHILI

Many days of laughter are wiped away by one moment of mourning – UGANDAN

Where one mourns [for] another, he mourns [for] himself – IGBO

What you recognise as deadly will not kill you – UGANDAN

DESPAIR & SORROW

Brooding deepens despair – SHONA

Do not prefer death to life in misfortune out of despair – ANCIENT EGYPTIAN

Hope is not equal to despair – MAASAI

Sorrow is like a precious treasure, shown only to friends – MALAGASY

Sorrows educate – THONGA

The grave diggers forget quickly but the bereaved doesn't – SUKUMA

One who has fallen: he understands how he should have acted (not to fall) – GANDA

DIFFERENCE

'Come see me' is one ting, but, 'Come lib [live] wid me,' is anuder [another] – JAMAICAN

Cheating and doing something by force are not the same – MAASAI

If your head is not like Tete's, you don't say, 'cut the figures on my hair like Tete's.' – TSHI

The left hand won't resemble the right hand – MAMPRUSSI

The penis does not know what the vagina thinks – IGBO

When the lizard and the rat jump into the water, the lizard's body dries, but the rat's [is] still wet – IGBO

You might give a loan whilst sitting, but to get it back you have to get up – GANDA

DIFFICULTY & DESPERATION

A difficult case is difficult to answer – TSHI

Hardship reveals personality – SWAHILI

If your part of the battle-field is covered with thorns, you do not leave your position and go to stand where the ground is good – TWI

Nothing is so difficult that diligence cannot conquer it – MALAGASY

Rain-fall mek [makes] sheep an'[d] goat a-wan [in one] pen – GUYANAN

The crooked board lets us see who is the real carpenter – TSHI

One who has lost his bow will look for it in a clay pot – SHONA

DILEMMA

A snake entering into the throat: if it is pulled it breaks, if it is released it goes [inside] – OROMO

Beauty is trouble, ugliness is tedious – IGBO

If you do not give you get robbed – HAYA

It is difficult to throw a stone at a lizard which is clinging to a pot – ASHANTI

One cannot both feast and become rich – ASHANTI

That man has two knives: the one with a handle is blunt and the sharp one has no handle – IGBO

The goat says the sickness of its owner is causing it [to] worry. If the sickness worsens, the healer asks for a goat as [a] sacrifice. If the owner gets well, a goat is required to celebrate recovery – YORUBA

There is weeping when separated, there is quarrelling when together – SWAHILI

DISAPPOINTMENT

E'[ve]ry day fishin'[g] day but no[t] e'ry day catch fish – BAHAMIAN

Ebery [every] day a fishing-day, but no[t] ebery day fe ketch [for catching] fish – JAMAICAN

The hard part of grinding is the first grinding, when that is done the rest is easy – HAUSA

'Let me see you do it!' makes the doing difficult – TSHI

It is easier to pull down than to build – SWAHILI

One who falls into a well will seize even the edge of a sword – HAUSA

If you chase away a coward and you don't give him room to flee, he shows you his strength – TSHI

Fire gives birth to ashes – **SUKUMA**

If something doesn't please you, it makes everything else bitter to you – **TSHI**

It is disappointing for one not to be loved by the person one loves – **YORUBA**

It's not only one man who suffers disappointment in the world – **MAMPRUSSI**

Not all flowers produce fruit – **SWAHILI**

The wishes of the heart never arrive – **KIKUYU**

To be disappointed is worse than not going at all – **TSHI**

She who keeps losing children doesn't invent names anymore – **UGANDAN**

DISCOVERY

A chicken can lie about her eggs but she cannot deceive about her chicks – **SURINAMESE**

A cough and love cannot be hidden – **TSONGA**

Ebery man hones' till de day him ketch – **JAMAICAN**
Every man is honest till the day he is caught.

She who asks does not go wrong, but her secret is dug up – **HAUSA**

He who breaks wind is angry with him who hears – **FULANI**

Lie down and die, you will see who really loves you – **HAUSA**

To lose the way is to know the way – **SWAHILI**

What you do secretly, others see secretly – **TWI**

DISCRETION & INDISCRETION

Dirty clothes are washed in the backyard – **SWAHILI**

Do not make home affairs known – **KIKUYU**

No ebery ting you yearry good fe talk – **JAMAICAN**
Not everything you hear is good to talk about.

Rabbit says, 'Drink everything, eat everything, but don't tell everything.' – **MARTINIQUE**

The wilderness has ears – **KAMBA**

There are troubles in the hut but the threshold covers them up – **MAMPRUSSI**

You can't kiss your back, and you can't speak out all things – **OROMO**

DOMINANCE

Annancy [the spider-man of myth] rope tie him massa [master]. [to overreach oneself] – **CARIBBEAN**

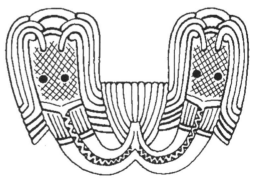

You nourish an orphan leopard; when its claws become strong it springs upon you – MONGO

Rear a python and it will swallow you – LOZI

Receive a dog and it will bite you – TSONGA

DRINKING & DRUNKENNESS

Drunken' man talk de [the] trut'[h] – JAMAICAN

Wha'[t] a sober heart conceal a drunken tongue reveal – BAJAN

When a cock gets drunk it forgets about the hawk – TSHI

When de rum a in, de wit a out – JAMAICAN
When the rum is in, the wit is out.

By not receiving any beer you didn't receive any drunkenness – UGANDAN

A thief goes with thieves, a drunkard with drunkards – SWAHILI

He that is drunk with wine gets sober, he that is drunk with wealth does not – SWAHILI

Beat a dog and you'll be hearing from its owner – HAITIAN

Gun no know he own massa [master] – GUYANAN

The Agada (short sword) does not know the head of the blacksmith who made it – YORUBA

The puppy feels big at his owner's front door – HAITIAN

Tree look ebber so soun'; woodpecker know wha' fe do wid him – JAMAICAN
The tree looks ever so sound; the woodpecker knows what to do with him.

You are the stone, I am the coconut – SWAHILI

DOUBLE-EDGEDNESS

A knife does not know its owner – MONGO

The key that opens is also the key that locks – KONGO

The sword shows no respect for its maker – YORUBA

The teeth that laugh are also those that bite – HAUSA

E

It is easy to cut to pieces a dead elephant – **YORUBA**

EASE

Bald head soon shabe [shaved] – **JAMAICAN**

Climbing [up] is easier than climbing down – **UGANDAN**

Once the lid is off the honey jar, anyone can eat her fill – **MALAGASY**

That which is quickly acquired is easily lost – **KIKUYU**

The song which is not difficult to sing will not be difficult to echo – **YORUBA**

When a long palm tree falls down, an old woman can climb it – **IGBO**

It is not difficult to shave the head of a sleeping child – **EWE**

The stick that is in your hand is the one you can count on to help you – **HAITIAN**

EATING & FOOD

A feast is good when someone [else] gives it – **IGBO**

A load of food is not burdensome – **OVAMBO**

Eat to live, don't live to eat – **HAITIAN**

He who cooked the food cooked well, she who ate it does better – **IGBO**

Only those who don't eat it smell the odour of the genet cat – **KAONDE**

The throat has no sorrow (you must eat even in time of trouble) – **THONGA**

E

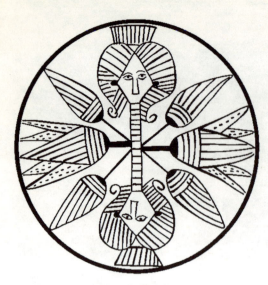

As we teach a child, so she learns – JABO

He who does not ask a question learns nothing – SWAHILI

She who studies goes on learning – SWAHILI

It's harder to teach than to learn – HAITIAN

Learning is the light that leads into everything lovely – SWAHILI

Man pay dear fe larn sometime' – JAMAICAN
A man pays dearly to learn sometimes.

To come out of one's house means learning – KIKUYU

Wealth, if you use it, comes to an end; learning, if you use it, increases – SWAHILI

There is no god like the throat: it takes sacrifices daily – NIGERIAN

What one won't eat alone, one will eat when mixed with other food – LAMBA

The sweetness of the meat depends on eating it – LAMBA

De cos' tek way from de tas'e – JAMAICAN
The cost takes away from the taste.

If the lizard were good to eat, it would not be so common – HAITIAN

EDUCATION

Children have no wisdom, kindness or love. [i.e. they need to learn these] – SWAHILI

Education has no end – SWAHILI

Education is the work of your entire life – HAITIAN

Even an ox can learn if well taught – NAMIBIAN

What de good a [of] education if him got no sense? – JAMAICAN

A learned person is she who has been told – KIKUYU

EFFORT

A new thing does not come to she who sits, but to she who travels – SHONA

An untouched drum does not speak – JABO

Bearing bends the neck of the banana tree [effort is costly] – KIKUYU

Big tree no [isn't] cut down wid [with] one blow – JAMAICAN

Dry water reeds, light as they are, begin to feel heavy on a long journey – LUYIA

Efforts and capabilities are not the same – MAASAI

Hand plow can't make furrows by itself – AFRICAN-AMERICAN

She who has not reached her destination never gets tired – **LUYIA**

If one does not know what to do, she does what she knows – **IGBO**

If you do not gather firewood you cannot keep warm – **OVAMBO**

If you do not rise when you do not want to, you will not arrive when you want to – **FULANI**

If you do not try to shoot you hit nothing – **OVAMBO**

If you do not want to go to the forest, do not expect the wild boar to come to you – **MALAGASY**

If you send no one to the market, the market will send no one to you – **YORUBA**

If you try your best you come out victorious – **TSHI**

'I'm tired' isn't laziness – **MAMPRUSSI**

Leaning against a full granary will not help a hungry man – **FULFULDE**

Progress depends on one's efforts – **HAYA**

Rest cannot shorten the way; going ahead does – **TSONGA**

Resting is not attaining – **GANDA**

Search much to get a little – **MAMPRUSSI**

Some stones are pretty when worn as necklaces but who is going to bore the hole in them? – **IGBO**

Striving is not getting – **SWAHILI**

Talkin'[g] [a]'bout fire doesn't boil the pot – **AFRICAN-AMERICAN**

That which is near is reached by she who stretches out her arm – **PEDI**

The bird will not fly into your arrow – **OVAMBO**

The blade of the hoe does not wear out for nothing – **ACHOLI**

The chicken that scratches brings out the worm – **SHERBRO**

The dog that searches every stone will never be without a bone – **NAMIBIAN**

The hare will not follow the dog – **OVAMBO**

The land is worth only so much as the person who works it – **HAITIAN**

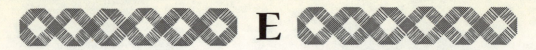

The ox that runs ahead is the one who drinks clear water – **HAITIAN**

To obtain good things you have to go and look for them – **GANDA**

What grows on its own is a forest; a field grows when it sees its master – **SHONA**

When fortune knocks at the door, you have to open the door yourself – **SWAHILI**

Who seeks, finds – **IGBO**

Whoever catches a hare has to run for it – **HAUSA**

Without overcoming bees you cannot get honey – **SWAHILI**

You move around and defeat him who will not leave his house – **OVAMBO**

Ain't no use askin'[g] the cow to pour you a glass of milk – **AFRICAN-AMERICAN**

EMOTIONS

A lame of heart is not a lame of leg: he cannot be recognised – **KIKUYU**

If you allow your emotions to rule you, you are lost – **TSHI**

The cry of alarm of the heart is not answered by anyone – **NDEBELE**

The heart is a thick forest which cannot be penetrated by anybody – **KIKUYU**

What can be expected to be dropped is held in the hands, but what is in the heart I shall die with – **SHONA**

Fire begets ashes – **TSONGA**

ENDING

De [the] longest day does bring home night – **BAJAN**

De langes' pray got a amen – **GUYANAN**
The longest prayer has an amen.

Even though a path is long, it comes to an end – **MAMPRUSSI**

Fus' laugh no laugh, a las' laugh a de laugh – **JAMAICAN**
The first laugh is no laugh, it's the last laugh that is the laugh.

Leaps and bounds and measured paces all end at the seashore – **TSHI**

The thing which was lost appears; enquiry ceases – **MONGO**

What is coming to an end is no longer important – **GANDA**

When the corpse is buried it ceases to smell – **IGBO**

Where the runner ends, there the walker will end – **IGBO**

ENDURANCE

De race no fe who can run but fe who run a
de end – JAMAICAN
The race is not for who can run but for who can run to the end.

If the animal is tied up for three years, he
does not say on the last day of his captivity
'The string is too tight today.' – TWI

If the dog didn't die in a year, it's not going to
die in a day – HAITIAN

That which the sun cannot dry up, the moon
will not dry it up – IGBO

The millipede crushed under the foot has not
frowned, yet she that did the crushing
frowns – IGBO

The patient has sometimes to bear
indignities in her treatment – TWI

ENEMIES

A leopard is not tied together with a goat –
ZULU

A man's friends are as many as his enemies –
TSWANA

Because a person hates you, that does not
prevent you getting what you want – HAUSA

Better an intelligent enemy than a stupid
friend – SWAHILI

Both the hawk and the fowl do not go to the
same market – IGBO

Do not whirl a snake in the air when you have
killed it; the ones which remain in their holes
see you – THONGA

Fear the person who is near you – TSHI

Fire and gunpowder do not sleep together –
ASHANTI

He who has not is the enemy of him who has
– SWAHILI

One who pursues you won't leave you unhurt
– UGANDAN

If a person hate you, gib [give] you fork fe [to]
drink soup – JAMAICAN

If a tree has many cuts it falls – KAONDE

If neyger [nigger] hate you, him gi'[ve] you
basket fe carry water; but if you cleber
[clever], you put plantain-leaf a [at the]
bottom – JAMAICAN

It's better that you kill your enemy than let your enemy kill you – **HAITIAN**

Know your enemy – **SWAHILI**

One does not bless the enemy – **TSHI**

One thinks (worries) more about enemies than she thinks about her friends – **HAITIAN**

People who fight on the ground should not go up the tree together – **OROMO**

Rising early to greet an enemy is a poor game – **HAUSA**

Spider an' fly no make bargain – **BAHAMIAN**

The bully bleeds the most – **LUYIA**

The cat is not at home: because of that the mice are playing – **HAUSA**

The cockroach never wins its cause when the chicken is judge – **HAITIAN**

The death of leopards is the safety of goats – **OROMO**

The enemy I know is better than the one I do not know – **KIKUYU**

The person who is not on good terms with you should not be sent into the bush to collect herbs for you when you are ill – **TWI**

The prayer of the fowl does not reach the kite – **SWAHILI**

The worm don't see nothing pretty in the robin's song – **AFRICAN-AMERICAN**

Wen cack roach mek dance, e no invite fowl – **CREOLE (BELIZE)**
When the cockroach holds a dance he doesn't ask [i.e. invite] the fowl.

What hen joins the council of cats? – **FULANI**

When news comes of your enemy's death say, 'This is his second time.' (As I had already dismissed him as dead for me) – **UGANDAN**

Where the dog is the monkey will not be – **MAMPRUSSI**

You bes' frien: da you wors' enemy – **CREOLE (BELIZE)**
Your best friend: that's your worst enemy.

Your enemy escorts your debtor – **HAYA**

Your friend is your enemy – **SWAHILI**

ENVIRONMENT

A child brought up where there is always dancing cannot fail to dance – **NYANJA**

E

As the crab is near the stream, it understands the language of the stream – **TWI**

At the home of the fiddler everyone knows how to dance – **HAITIAN**

Big ship need deep water – **JAMAICAN**

However deep the water the frog sees to the bottom of it – **HAUSA**

If a crocodile deserts the water, it will find itself on a spear – **BURA**

If a frog is thrown into water it doesn't die – **SWAHILI**

If the melon lies in one place, it ripens – **TWI**

The environment is the beginning of success – **SWAHILI**

The strength of a fish is in the water – **SHONA**

Two stick grow da [in the] bush; one grow straight, one grow crooked – **CREOLE (BELIZE)**

When a yam doesn't grow well, we don't blame it; it is because of the soil – **TSHI**

EQUALITY & INEQUALITY

Equality is spiritual – **SWAHILI**

A tree of your height cannot shade you – **SWAHILI**

God created the rich and the poor – **TSHI**

He that does not fear a bull must be a bull himself – **SWAHILI**

An egg cannot fight with a stone – **BURA**

If you see one in the shade another is in the sun – **HAUSA**

Man knack iron, iron na a-feel am, iron knack man, man a-feel am – **GUYANAN**
A man knocks [strikes/runs into] iron, iron doesn't feel him, iron knocks a man, the man feels it.

Six do not fight with seven – **MONGO**

T'[h]ree silver fish can't mek [make] one Congo fish – **GUYANAN**

What a tall woman has hung up a short man cannot undo – **SUKUMA**

ESCAPE

Escaping with your reputation is better than escaping with your property – **HAUSA**

One whom they did not manage to catch will not fail to plead 'not guilty.' – **GANDA**

If thou drive a beast and give it no way, it turns upon thee – **GA**

It isn't ugly to run when one isn't strong enough to stay – **TRINIDADIAN**

To be able to discuss the accident means you have escaped – **SHONA**

Once the frog has extricated itself from the snake's jaws, the snake will never catch it again – HAITIAN

The animal that does not try to free itself (from the trap) will die – GANDA

EUROPEANS

Beware of French people who pretend to quarrel with each other: they will join together to fight you – MALAGASY

Don't tell the white man he has forgot his hat, he'll just say, 'Nigger, bring it here.' – AFRICAN-AMERICAN

The sweet-worded Englishman who finally hurts you – SUKUMA

If there had been no poverty in Europe, then the white man would not have come and spread his clothes in Africa – TSHI

Niggah forget, Bacra 'membah – GUYANAN
Nigger forget, Bacra [European] remember.

The white man has no kin. His kin is his money – TSONGA

The white man is a white man – TSONGA

They prevent us from getting red clay from the pit, and [yet] they do not use it – XHOSA

Wen black man teef thieves, e teef some; wen bakra teef, e teef all – CREOLE (BELIZE)
When black man thieves, he thieves some; when bakra [European] thieves, he thieves all.

When the white man is about to leave a garden for good, he wrecks it – YORUBA

EVIL

A vicious snake may bite its own tail – TSWANA

An evil that is self-inflicted is not the same as one inflicted by others (or: does not make you angry with others) – GANDA

Bad ting neba gat owner – CREOLE (BELIZE)
A bad thing never gets an owner.

De bwoy dat bad no wort' trashin' – JAMAICAN
The boy that's bad isn't worth thrashing.

One who has revealed evil has caused the truth to come out – SHONA

She who seeks evil finds it – KIKUYU

If you do something bad, you never forget it – TSHI

If you see wrongdoing or evil and say nothing against it, you become its victim – AFRICAN

One cannot remove the poison of the

crocodile, the snake, and the evil one – ANCIENT EGYPTIAN

People are consumed by evil because of keeping close to it, but not because of keeping away from it – KIKUYU

Talk ob de debil an you heah he wings – GUYANAN
Talk of the devil and you hear his wings.

The evil-doer is ever anxious – YORUBA

When a man is setting out to do evil, advice is a joke to him – TSHI

You continue to see good, don't forget evil – MONGO

Yuh [you] got one more trick dan [than] de devil – BAJAN

EXAMPLE

A tree which is straight supports the crooked tree – TSHI

An adulterer gets his wife ravished – KIKUYU

Examples have children – TSHI

If a person has met their death by stumbling, you do not run to attend the funeral – TSHI

If the leader does not walk straight, those who follow him will do the same – TSONGA

If you carry your baby and you steal, you show it how to do so – UGANDAN

Someone sees when someone else acts – MAMPRUSSI

The dead gazelle teaches the live gazelle – CHAGGA

EXCESS & MEASURE

A child that cries much: nobody knows when she has been beaten badly – IGBO

Dipping one finger in the pot doesn't finish off the honey – UGANDAN

Exaggerated love brings exaggerated hatred – OROMO

If a bow is drawn too tight it will break – OVAMBO

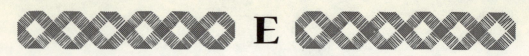
EXPERIENCE

'It happened to me before' prompted an old fowl to take to its heels at the sight of a hawk – **YORUBA**

'Let-it-cool-down' had already burnt itself – **SHONA**

A bad experience is a teaching to you – **HAYA**

A satisfied person does not know what a hungry one feels – **FULANI**

A travelled child knows better than the old man who sits at home – **IGBO**

A travelling baby tied on the back of her mother does not know that trekking is tiresome – **IGBO**

An orphan will soon be an adult – **NAMIBIAN**

Anything bad is only detected by tasting – **KIKUYU**

Appetite comes by tasting – **UGANDAN**

Choking will teach you to chew properly; falling will teach you to walk properly – **MALAGASY**

Fish a deep water no know how fish a riberside feel – **JAMAICAN**
The fish in deep water doesn't know how the fish at the riverside feels.

If one over-feasts, one must over-work – **IGBO**

If one person eats all the honey, he is sure to get a belly-ache – **TSHI**

If you pick up too much, some falls down – **TSHI**

No one knocks an old woman [down] to see where she will fall – **TSHI**

To do to much to obtain a thing makes one miss it – **FULFULDE**

Too heavy a bundle breaks the back of the wood-gatherer – **UGANDAN**

Too much a [of] one t'ing good fo'[r] not'in' – **CREOLE (BELIZE)**

We do not cut open someone's head to see what is in it – **TSHI**

When bud [bird] fly too fas'[t] him pass him nes'[t] – **JAMAICAN**

Full belly man na [doesn't] know wha'[t] hungry belly a-suffer – **GUYANAN**

He who eats with a stick does not know that he who eats with the fingers gets scalded – **KIKUYU**

She who knows the path is she who travels it – **ZULU**

She who says, 'It is excellent,' must have tasted it – **HAYA**

He whom a serpent has bitten dreads a slow-worm – **OJI**

I shall believe they are zebras when I see their stripes – **TSWANA**

If the food is delicious the tongue knows – **TSHI**

If the iguana comes out of the river to say that the crocodile is ill, nobody doubts it – **TWI**

If you don't carry me, you won't know how heavy I am – **MAMPRUSSI**

If you've had the sickness, you know the remedy – **HAITIAN**

It's before the drum that one learns to know the samba – **HAITIAN**

Loose-goat na [doesn't] a-feel wha'[t] tie-goat a-feel – **GUYANAN**

Man a sea no know how man a lan' dey feel – **JAMAICAN**
The man at sea doesn't know how the man on land feels.

Never give up what you have seen for what you have heard – **SWAHILI**

New broom sweep clean, but de ole [old] broom know de carner [corner] – **JAMAICAN**

Not until we have fallen do we know how to re-arrange our burden – **YORUBA**

One single place gives no experience – **GANDA**

One who does not move about knows very little – **HAYA**

One who has been pricked by a thorn values shoes – **SWAHILI**

One who has never had a flogging will not pay any attention when you merely tell him to stop – **HAUSA**

One who says, "I have never seen such a thing," is not yet an adult – SWAHILI

Rocktone a riber no know wha' rocktone a roadside a feel – JAMAICAN
The stone in the river doesn't know what the stone on the roadside feels.

Seeing for oneself is different from being told – KIKUYU

Staying in a place and living there are different – IGBO

That which bit me yesterday and hurt me, does not crawl over me a second time – SWAHILI

The damaged net teaches the bush fowl a lesson – YORUBA

The deaf who does not hear when rain is threatening, will know when it drops on her – IGBO

The lame knows how to fall – LUYIA

The macaco (monkey) doesn't climb up the (thorny) acacia tree two times – HAITIAN

The one holds the pot knows how hot it is – HAITIAN

One who does not eat it does not know its sweetness – GANDA

The one who is born before you sees the sun before you – SWAHILI

The person who has tasted it is the one who may praise it – LUYIA

The pregnant woman is not afraid of her husband's penis – OVAMBO

The unprotected town has never had enemies – NAMIBIAN

There is gain even in stupidity – TSHI

Those who climb with their teeth know trees with bitter barks – NIGERIAN

To be told is not to see – SWAHILI

To know a jungle is to spend a day in it – KIKUYU

To see once is to see twice – ZULU

What is in the yams that a knife doesn't know? – TEMNE

What is old for one may be new for another – SHONA

What made one alert is what happened before – SHONA

What one sees with one's eyes is not what one hears from another's tongue – **KIKUYU**

When a person falls, she becomes acquainted with the nature of the ground – **IGBO**

When a twig hits you in the eye it says 'watch out.' – **UGANDAN**

When you have been bitten by a snake you flee from a worm – **BASA**

Who is not taught by her mother will be taught by the world – **SWAHILI**

Will you venture on the coals a second time? – **TSWANA**

You make a new arrow by comparing it to an old one – **TSHI**

You must go to the market to know what business is like at the market – **OROMO**

We begin by being foolish and we become wise by experience – **MAASAI**

EXPERTISE

An old woman is not old in a song she dances well – **NIGERIAN**

Expertise is accepted when it comes from experts – **SHONA**

Fishing in deep water requires skill – **SWAHILI**

It is not the trap that counts, but the art of trapping – **KIKUYU**

Leave the handling of the gun to the hunter – **NAMIBIAN**

Nobody can do what an expert cannot do – **SHONA**

Nobody will deceive a baboon by tricks – **OJI**

Smooth seas do not make skilful mariners – **SWAHILI**

The better [the] swimmer, the greater the chances of getting drowned – **HAITIAN**

The task that scares away a stranger is the host's special pastime – **NIGERIAN**

You can speak about spears only with one who has fought with them – **GANDA**

E

When jackass fas' dem tek him fe draw cart –
JAMAICAN
When the jackass is fast they take him to draw the cart.

You make me out to be a dhow [a sea vessel] and you to be the rudder – **SWAHILI**

EXPRESSION

A child that does not cry dies in the sling-cradle – **SHONA**

A deaf and dumb person's dream remains in their head – **TSHI**

Explain your need, so you get what you need – **SWAHILI**

If you need something, better say so; keeping silent you will not get it – **SHONA**

Knowing and not being able to say – **MAMPRUSSI**

That which did not shout for help but waited patiently died in the trap – **LUYIA**

The chicken says she cries to let the public know her condition, not that her enemy will release her – **IGBO**

The dog's dream remains in the dog's heart – **HAITIAN**

We say what the elder has said, not what she is thinking – **TSHI**

You shouldn't hold back the voice of your complaint and then expect to be acquitted – **TSHI**

EXPLOITATION

A hass [horse's] good heart mek [makes] man a-ride am [him] as he like – **GUYANAN**

A hill that doesn't wish to be trodden on must not grow edible mushrooms – **MENDE**

He makes a ladder of other people's backs – **TSWANA**

The good taste of the date prevents it from growing – **FULFULDE**

The labourer cultivates in the sun, his master eats in the shade – **SWAHILI**

The pot cooks the food and does not eat it – **KIKUYU**

The sower is one person, the harvester is another – **SUKUMA**

F

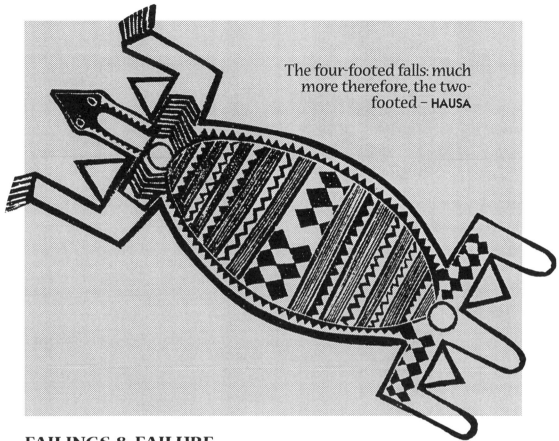

The four-footed falls; much more therefore, the two-footed – HAUSA

FAILINGS & FAILURE

As the tree faces, so does it fall – SUKUMA

The ox falls in spite of its four legs – NANDI

A good cook, but a poor distributor – SUKUMA

Having choked you are able to chew; having fallen you are able to walk – MALAGASY

He who praises you for climbing well calls you a cripple when you fall – GANDA

I will no longer water a fig tree which does not sprout – OVAMBO

The needle is well threaded but does not sew – SWAHILI

When a ship is broken (wrecked), the accident does not prevent others from sailing – MARTINIQUE

FAIRNESS & IMPARTIALITY

'Hit me but I must not hit you,' is no game at all – TSHI

Partnership in the trap, share of the meat – MONGO

Swap and change ent [isn't] nuh [no] robbery – BAJAN

When one is treated as others [have] been treated, her mind will be cool – IGBO

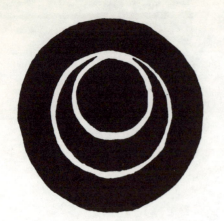

Ear, hear the other side of the question before you decide – YORUBA

The leopard licks all its spots, black and white – NDEBELE

The rain does not befriend anybody; it falls on anyone it meets outside – YORUBA

It is a bad doorway that lets bad and good enter – GANDA

The grass-torch that burns a bad house, also burns a good one – GANDA

The sword does not discriminate between the blacksmith's head and other heads – YORUBA

A good case is not difficult to state – TSHI

Do not be afraid to do that in which you are right – ANCIENT EGYPTIAN

He who has carved his walking-stick fights for it – UGANDAN

Let her who shook the fruit down pick them too – OVAMBO

FAMILIARITY

A cow-herd does not fear a cow – GA

A gunsmith (hunter) does not fear the mysteries of the forest – SHONA

A river drowns the one who can swim – KIKUYU

An everyday path has no signpost – SWAHILI

Better than the angel whom one does not know is the Satan whom one knows – GURAGE

Ebery [every] man know weh [where] he own house a-leak – GUYANAN

Familiarity to the eye breeds contempt – HAUSA

Houses which are close together, burn together – SWAHILI

It is only the knife that knows the heart of the yam – HAITIAN

It is the still water that drowns a man – TWI

It's the hut you know that you go in while it's dark – MAMPRUSSI

It's the knife that knows what's in the heart of the pumpkin – MARTINIQUE

People know each other better on a journey – TSWANA

Rotten meat cannot make a hyena sick – FULFULDE

So it is with a thing you are acquainted with: the rat does not knock its head against the darkest corner in the house – **GANDA**

The cow is milked by one who knows it – **ZULU**

The familiar will not be feared – **FULANI**

The fish don't see the water – **HAITIAN**

The hand does not miss its way into the mouth in the dark – **EWE**

The person who knows the ford well is the one whom the crocodile seizes – **HAUSA**

The one who serves the food knows the pot – **TSONGA**

The pit into which a stranger falls, an local person already knows – **AFRICAN**

The road by which you are accustomed to pass cannot be mistaken – **MONGO**

The thorn-eating animal knows how to chew them – **UGANDAN**

What affects the penis will affect the vagina – **IGBO**

What is in the yam that a knife does not know? – **TEMNE**

What one is used to cannot harm one – **YORUBA**

When a crab runs away it flees towards the sea – **ASHANTI**

FAMILY

[A] faithful friend is never better than a sister – **IGBO**

A brother is born for adversity – **SOUTHERN AFRICA**

A brotherly staff does not break – **EWE**

A cousin does not ask and is not refused anything – **KIKUYU**

A man's brother should not be thirsty when the man is carrying water on his head – **IGBO**

Anger towards a sister is only flesh deep not bone deep – **IGBO**

As long as my brother does not desist from stealing, I do not desist from restraining him – **ANCIENT EGYPTIAN**

Don't abandon your family and friends for strangers – **HAITIAN**

If Komu has it, Kaigu, his brother, has it too – **KIKUYU**

If the bangle is taken from the right hand and placed on the left hand, the bangle is still on the hand – YORUBA

If the thief is not ashamed, his sister will be ashamed – IGBO

If your child goes to the rubbish heap and a snake bites her, you do not cut off that part of the body, but you apply medicine to it – TSHI

If your hand gets soiled, you do not cut it off – SWAHILI

Impatience with your brother is in the flesh, it doesn't reach the bone – MAMPRUSSI

It's your own people who tell you the truth – HAITIAN

Jaybird don't rob his own nest – AFRICAN-AMERICAN

Mother carry me, I too will carry you – BEMBA

One cannot hear [a] brother's cry and say [one] is busy – IGBO

Oneness (through blood) cannot be severed – KIKUYU

The cow licks her own calf only – GANDA

The fence around a house conceals the secrets of a household – TWI

The flour not in your mother's hut is ashes – UGANDAN

There is no brother in the family except the brother who is kindhearted – ANCIENT EGYPTIAN

Things of the family [family affairs] should not be escorted outside the boundary of the homestead – KIKUYU

If the father is good, the child will be good – HAITIAN

What happens in the family is not for outsiders – GANDA

When your brother can't give you milk he begs it from others for you – UGANDAN

One finger gashed - all the fingers are covered with blood – NKUNDU

FATE

He who refuses his fate...it waits for him ahead – SWAHILI

If God has not decreed your death, you don't die – TSHI

No plant comes to flower but to wither – SOUTHERN AFRICA

The animal that is coming [i.e. fated] to be killed, does not hear the hunter cough – TSHI

The destiny the Supreme Being has assigned to you cannot be avoided – ASHANTI

What happened to the old winnowing tray will happen to the new one – **SWAHILI**

For everyone there is an appointed time – **ANCIENT EGYPTIAN**

What's destined to be yours, no one can take away from you – **HAITIAN**

FAULTS

A bag that has a hole can never be filled – **MAASAI**

De bes a field mus' hab weed – **JAMAICAN**
The best of fields must have weeds.

Ebery [every] house hab [have] him dirty corner – **JAMAICAN**

Faults are like a hill, you mount on your own and see other people's – **HAUSA**

First sweep your own house before you despise someone else's – **LUYIA**

He who does not see his own vices...should not take notice of the faults of his companions – **SWAHILI**

If a monkey fails to climb a tree, the tree must have a defect – **SWAHILI**

No one is free from faeces – **IGBO**

One's own open wound does not smell – **KIKUYU**

Parson can' preach wid dutty collar for all yeye dey 'pon him – **JAMAICAN**
The parson can't preach with a dirty collar for all eyes are upon him.

The ape sees not his own hinder parts, he sees his neighbour's – **SWAHILI**

The eye does not see itself – **TSONGA**

The index-finger does not point to itself – **SHONA**

The road is fair but crooked – **EFIK**

The swimmer doesn't see his own back – **HO**

We can see the backs of other people's heads, and other people can see the back of ours – **YORUBA**

You are always straightening other people's fences; your own are leaning – **OVAMBO**

You mend only a thing that is not good – **OJI**

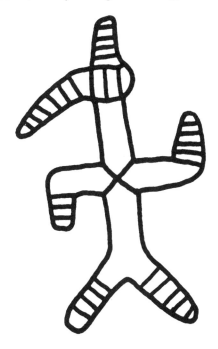

65

F

She who fears harm escapes all harm –
ANCIENT EGYPTIAN

One who is afraid of bees will not eat their
honey – OVAMBO

He who is scared of a hyena's howling is he
who has smeared himself with fat – SHONA

If your neighbour cheats you and you don't
cheat her, it means you fear her – TSHI

People run to avoid the snake, and the snake
runs to avoid human beings – YORUBA

Rejoice over the fearful and cry for the
fearless – KAONDE

The saying is: 'Fear has long life,' and not,
'courage has long life.' – TSHI

When fear enters, truth escapes – SWAHILI

FAVOUR

Being in the giver's good graces is worth
more than an outstretched hand – HAUSA

Favours enslave – SWAHILI

She who does favours will receive favours –
HAITIAN

He who eats with his mother will not cry for
scrapings – HAUSA

If your sister is in the group of singing girls,
your name always comes into the song – TSHI

The prince is never guilty in his father's court
– IGBO

The son of the god of thunder does not die of
lightning – EWE

When your sister is in heaven, it is not likely
you will go to hell – IGBO

FEAR

A cautious person will never learn how to
swim – OROMO

Fear the one you don't know until you come
to know him – SWAHILI

One who back-bites you fears you – LUYIA

FIGHTING & VIOLENCE

Not to fight is better than fighting and
making it up – ANGASS

Only by fighting can the better man be found
out – HAUSA

To fight once shows bravery, but to fight all
the time is stupid – OROMO

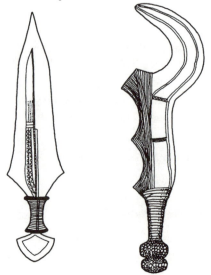

He who delights in the knife will die by the knife – BEMBA

A blow is repaid by the like of it, and all that is achieved is a hitting – ANCIENT EGYPTIAN

When a father beats his child, he is likely to beat also its mother (who wants to protect the child) – GANDA

If you have enemies then travel with your spear – NAMIBIAN

If he has thrown the only spear he had at you it means that he doesn't fear you – UGANDAN

When brothers fight each other, don't intervene – UGANDAN

FIRE

A small fire destroys a big forest – HAYA

Do not kindle a fire that you cannot put out – SWAHILI

Fire is not extinguished by another fire – KIKUYU

If fire should break out on the road leading to the stream, where shall we go [for water]? – TEMNE

The ashes are the children of the fire – BURA

The eye that sees smoke looks for fire – HAUSA

One who is lying by the fire knows how it burns – TSHI

FLEXIBILITY

Better fall like a basket than like an earthen dish – LUYIA

If man na ben' he back, he go jam he head a-post – GUYANAN
If a man doesn't bend his back he will jam [i.e. strike] his head against the door-post.

The bending tree isn't broken by the wind – SUKUMA

The small finger is not difficult to bend, nor difficult to straighten – TSHI

Dere is many way fe choke darg widout put rope roun' him neck – JAMAICAN
There are many ways to choke a dog without putting a rope round his neck.

More way fuh [to] hang dog dan [than] tie rope round 'e [his] neck – BAJAN

Plenty way deh fo' choke daag widout hangin' rope roun' he neck – GUYANAN
There are plenty of ways to choke a dog without hanging a rope round his neck.

Rice is one, but there are many ways of cooking – SWAHILI

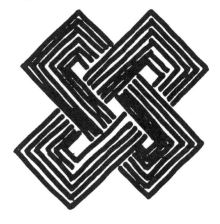

FOLLY

A chicken having been delivered from death (i.e. from the hawk) by being shut up, complained because it was not allowed to feed openly on the dust-heap – YORUBA

A cracked plate laughs at a broken one – SHONA

A leopard is chasing us and do you ask me: 'Is it a male or female?' – TEMNE

A pot laughs at potsherd[s] [shattered pots] – GIRIAMA

A simpleton [throws] a blow at the porcupine – MAMPRUSSI

Are you teaching a monkey the way to climb? – TSWANA

Do not be like the hedgehog who fears the lantern but not the lightning – MALAGASY

Foolishness can't be treated – SUKUMA

He goes for a mamba in its hole – ZULU

She has a spoon but her hand is burnt – FULANI

He lived with priests and died without being baptised – HAITIAN

If a person goes in the bush and is pricked by a thorn while there is a path, he wanted it – MAMPRUSSI

If the cutlass strikes a rock, it pays (suffers) – TSHI

'If you are given bread for foolishness you may despise instruction – ANCIENT EGYPTIAN

If you throw a stone in a crowded market, you are liable to hit your relative – YORUBA

In a pool with crocodiles, you swim only once – SHONA

Insanity can be treated, but not foolishness – SUKUMA

It is the fool's sheep that breaks loose twice – IGBO

Never ask to be told the obvious – KURIA

No one should draw water from the spring in order to supply the river – YORUBA

One who cannot pick up an ant and wants to pick up an elephant will someday see his folly – JABO

The faggot in the itara (drying rack) laughs at the one in the fire – KIKUYU

The fool-hardy learns by the flow of blood – ZULU

The journey of folly has to be travelled a second time – **BONDEI**

The silly dog hunts an elephant – **UGANDAN**

When advised, the silly person says, 'They hate me.' – **UGANDAN**

When in the fold ye have put a leopard, the regret of it never ends – **SWAHILI**

While the forest burns the young monkey laughs – **UGANDAN**

You bathe and you don't change your clothes – **HAITIAN**

You have cast away your own for that which you are not sure of – **XHOSA**

What is sensible today may be madness another time – **YORUBA**

FOOLS

A fool is the wise woman's ladder – **ZULU**

A fool laughs at himself – **OVAMBO**

A fool repeatedly brings his case back to the court – **KIKUYU**

A fool who has eighty cents thinks that everything costs eighty cents – **MALAGASY**

A person that buys an ox by the foot-mark – **NYIKA**

A man no know he own want is a fool – **GUYANAN**
A man who doesn't know his own want [i.e. needs] is a fool.

A self-made fool is worse than a natural one – **KIKUYU**

A warning to the wise is a blessing, to the fool an insult – **SWAHILI**

All fool can talk, but na [not] all can heah [hear] – **GUYANAN**

Another's instruction does not enter the

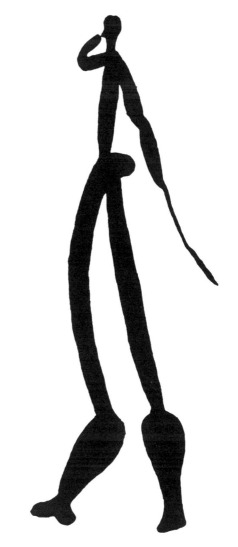

heart of the fool; what is in his heart is in his heart – **ANCIENT EGYPTIAN**

Big promise mek [makes] fool merry – **JAMAICAN**

By the time the fool learns the game, the players have dispersed – **IGBO**

De wises'[t] man is sometime'[s] [a] fool – **JAMAICAN**

Do not argue with a fool, for people will not be able to tell between the two of you – **IGBO**

69

Do not instruct a fool, lest he hate you –
ANCIENT EGYPTIAN

Don't show the unbaked pot to a fool –
UGANDAN

Fool di talk but no fool dis listen – CREOLE
(BELIZE)
The fool talks but it's no fool that listens.

Fools are treasures for the cunning – TSWANA

God does not help a fool – OVAMBO

He is a fool who does not know his equal –
IGBO

One who claps hands for a fool to dance is no
better than the fool – YORUBA

He who thinks that he is clever is a fool –
SWAHILI

If a foolish person is insulted in secret, he will
insult himself in public. [i.e. in publicly
denouncing the insult] – OROMO

If fool no go a market, bad somet[h]in[g]
nebber [never] sell – JAMAICAN

If one advises a fool, it seems to him that one
has insulted him – GURAGE

If the speaker is a fool, the listener is no fool –
HAUSA

If you demand payment for a debt from a
fool, you have put off the payment of your
debt – TSHI

If you play with a fool you become a fool – TSHI

In a fight with a fool it is the wise man who
quits – MALAGASY

It is difficult to recognize a fool who is also a
proprietor – TSWANA

It is the fool who says, 'They mean my friend,
they don't mean me.' – TSHI

It is the fool whose own garden eggs [egg-
plants/aubergines] are plucked and sold to
him – TSHI

Lawyer house buil'[t] [u]'pon fool head –
JAMAICAN

One cannot teach wisdom to a fool – OVAMBO

One fool mek [makes] many – GUYANAN

Only fool put puss [cat] fe [to] watch milk –
JAMAICAN

The clever one takes one penny worth of gold
dust and receives from the hand of the fool
gold dust of the value of a pound – ASHANTI

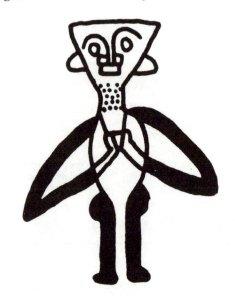

The counsel that occurs to the fool is weightless like the wind – ANCIENT EGYPTIAN

The evil that befalls the fool, his belly and his phallus bring it – ANCIENT EGYPTIAN

The fool and the paper do not let go what one made them hold – GURAGE

The fool beaten up at a beer party takes it out on his wife – UGANDAN

The fool doubts what the wise woman does not doubt – IGBO

The fool is killed by what belongs to himself – KIKUYU

The fool never grows old, never changes – SUKUMA

[The] inheritance of fools is eaten by the wise – NDEBELE

The rivalry of a fool is inability to recognise his superior – HAUSA

The wise one does not say that what she says is the final word, but the fool insists – SHONA

To approach a fool is to flee him – ANCIENT EGYPTIAN

'Tomorra' a de burden a de fool – JAMAICAN
'Tomorrow' is the burden [i.e. refrain] of the fool.

What the market people heard, the fool hides from his wife at home – OROMO

"What they do insults me," says the fool when one teaches him – ANCIENT EGYPTIAN

When a fool does not succeed in bleaching ebony he tries to blacken ivory – AMHARIC

When a fool is told a proverb, it has to be explained to him – TSHI

You follow fool, you fool you'[r]self – JAMAICAN

FORESIGHT

Darkness shows no wrong path to she who gets what she wants before dark – KIKUYU

Foresight spoils nothing – DUALA

Having left nothing, you will find nothing – RWANDA

If duck no leab [leave] pond, pond leab duck – JAMAICAN

If nothing has ever done you any harm, you will never have foresight – DUALA

If your neighbour's house burns, draw water for putting out the fire on yours – SWAHILI

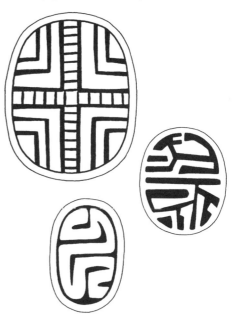

Nyam some, lef' some, 'member tomorra –
JAMAICAN
Eat some, leave some, remember tomorrow.

She got pregnant and wanted meat so a
pregnant cow was killed for her. When she
gave birth, she wanted milk and there was
nothing to give her – **OROMO**

She who has given birth eats what she
cultivated during pregnancy – **UGANDAN**

She/he learns reconciliation before knowing
how to fight – **OROMO**

Sore-foot [lame] man start fe [to] go a market
from Friday night [i.e. the day before] –
JAMAICAN

That which is in the sea, go and wait for on
the beach – **SWAHILI**

The firewood gathered when you are healthy
warms you when you are sick – **UGANDAN**

The goat that climbs up the rocks must climb
down again – **GUYANAN**

Tomorrow's business one gets ready today –
SWAHILI

FORETHOUGHT

A melting ointment is sold before the sun
starts to shine – **BINI**

Before you start something, make sure you
can finish it – **HAITIAN**

Cricket with only one leg sets off early – **IGBO**

Do not sell your house and your income for
the sake of one day and then be poor forever
– **ANCIENT EGYPTIAN**

She who does not consider the outcome will
end with an 'If I had known.' – **SWAHILI**

He who doesn't look ahead falls behind –
HAITIAN

Lilly forethought sabe afta t'ought – **JAMAICAN**
A little forethought saves afterthought.

Nebbah t'row 'way to-day wha' you go want
tomorrow – **GUYANAN**
Never throw away today what you're going to want tomorrow.

Prepare now for the solution of tomorrow's
problems – **SWAHILI**

When you drink water, do not fill the well
with sand. Where will you drink tomorrow? –
TSONGA

When you think of running, think also about
getting tired – **HAITIAN**

Where one has seen a way of climbing up,
there might be no climbing down – **GANDA**

You will not be beaten when you think before
acting – **MAASAI**

F

FORGETTING

Rat a-fo'get, trap na fo'get – **GUYANAN**
Rat forgets, the trap doesn't forget.

To forget is the same as to throw away –
AFRICAN

The person who excreted it may forget it, but
the one who steps in it does not – **LUYIA**

The river that forgets its source will dry up –
YORUBA

The speaker may forget, but she who is
spoken to does not – **ILA**

The tongue forgets more than the ear –
UGANDAN

To forget is the same as to throw away –
AFRICAN

To trouble me is better than to forget me –
NUPE

When you think about forgetting someone,
that's thinking about him – **HAITIAN**

FORGIVENESS

A word of peace redeems a crime – **OVAMBO**

Forgiving is victory – **SWAHILI**

She that forgives gains the victory – **ZULU**

He who does not know how to forgive, let
him not expect to be forgiven – **SWAHILI**

One who forgives ends the quarrel – **YORUBA**

If you do not forgive a crime, you commit a
crime – **TWI**

FORTUNE

Ebery day debil help tief; wan day God mus'
help watchman – **GUYANAN**
Every day the devil helps the thief; one day God must help the
watchman.

Good fortune will not happen to you; good
fortune is given to him who seeks it – **ANCIENT
EGYPTIAN**

Green maize abounds at the houses of those
without teeth – **SHONA**

On the day the tortoise dresses well he never
meets his father-in-law – **NIGERIAN**

Perhaps you will eat a whole elephant and
nothing gets stuck in your throat, and then
you eat a fish and a bone gets stuck in your
throat – **TSHI**

When fortune knocks at the door, you have
to open the door yourself – **SWAHILI**

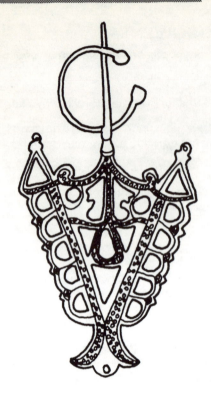

FRIENDS & FRIENDSHIP

A fond embrace doesn't necessarily mean a good friend – **HAITIAN**

A kind 'good morning' doesn't mean you're great friends – **HAITIAN**

One who is not friendly does not get assistance when he requires it – **HAYA**

The fact that people visit you often doesn't make them your friends – **HAITIAN**

Make to thyself a friend of one that is upright and righteous – **ANCIENT EGYPTIAN**

A powerful friend becomes a powerful enemy – **AMHARIC**

A wise person does not tell her friend everything about herself lest her secrets be divulged in a later quarrel – **NIGERIAN**

Among many friends there is one true friend – **TSHI**

Friends know you when you are prosperous and you know them when you are in adversity – **SWAHILI**

Friendship requires frequency [i.e. of visiting] – **KIKUYU**

Friendship with the ferryman right from the dry season means that when the rains come you will be the first to cross – **HAUSA**

Giving to your friend is not the same as throwing away, it is a reserve for the future – **SWAHILI**

She who does not advise you is not your friend – **OVAMBO**

Hold a true friend with both your hands – **KANURI / BORNU**

I know my friend, I don't know my friend's friend – **MAMPRUSSI**

If you are careful with your enemy once, be careful with your friend a thousand times – **SWAHILI**

If you wan' fe know you fren', lie down a roadside form drunk – **JAMAICAN**
If you want to know your friend, lie down at the roadside and pretend to be drunk.

It is easier to lose a friend than to find her again – **SWAHILI**

It is friendship that makes me dine in a friend's house; there is enough to eat in my own home – **NIGERIAN**

Lending money and loaning things kill[s] friendship – **GANDA**

Mek fren' when you no need dem – **JAMAICAN**
Make friends when you don't need them.

Money done [finished], frien'[d] done –
GUYANAN

One who gets tired of an old friendship will also get tired of a new one – **GANDA**

One who is quick to act in your favour is a real friend – **HAYA**

Promise get frien'; perform keep am – **GUYANAN**
Promise gets a friend; performance keeps him.

The house-bound child won't have friends –
UGANDAN

Too many friends seem like the legs of a crab: numerous and useless – **MALAGASY**

Too much love spoils the friendship – **KIKUYU**

When your friend throws your father to the ground, he throws away your friendship –
UGANDAN

Your friend is a relative – **OVAMBO**

Your friend weighs more than your brother –
OVAMBO

Don't make it a dog's friendship, to be broken over a bone – **MALAGASY**

Your smile should be more like the spring sun than the winter sun – **MALAGASY**

FUTILITY & IMPOTENCE

"I nearly killed the bird." No one can eat 'nearly' in a stew – **YORUBA**

A bachelor has no wife, so his penis [becomes] erect to do what? – **MAMPRUSSI**

A corpse, though you weep – **OVAMBO**

A dead person cannot see your tears –
MALAGASY

A thief who steals a bugle will find nowhere to blow it – **YORUBA**

Deaf ear gi'[ve] story-carrier trouble – **JAMAICAN**

Do not teach a fish to swim – **TSONGA**

Do not tie up a dog with a chain of sausages –
CREOLE LOUISIANA

Don't put an ornament over dirt – **MALAGASY**

She lights a fire in the wind – NDEBELE

He who spits towards the sky is spitting on his face – IGBO

I know how to shout a curse, but the thief is hard of hearing – TSHI

It is a shield of leaves – TSONGA

It is better to go in vain than to stay in vain – SWAHILI

It is futile to be afraid of crocodiles when your feet are already in the water – SHONA

It is of no use to wink in the dark – SHONA

No one goes to hide and then coughs – TSHI

The corpse that does not like where it is buried should get up and go – IGBO

The snake that bites the tortoise 'wastes' its teeth – IGBO

Though you talk sense to a deaf person theycannot hear you – OVAMBO

To pound water with a mortar is futile – KIKUYU

To strike a branch on which sits a bird that is on the point of flying only makes it fly the sooner – TEMNE

To take water to the river is a waste of time – HAYA

Walk fo' not'in' bettah dan si' down fo' not'in.' – GUYANAN
To walk for nothing is better than to sit down for nothing.

When you hear the raucous laugh of the hyena it's because it has seen one woman escorting another [i.e. it will eat them both] – UGANDAN

You have thrown a frog into the water – LUYIA

Your mother will not return though you may weep – OVAMBO

You can' tie darg wid link a sausage – JAMAICAN
You can't tie a dog with a link made of sausages.

FUTURE

'Hasn't yet got' may ever get – MAMPRUSSI

To-day fo'[r] you, to-morrow fo' me – GUYANAN

Today and tomorrow are two different things – HAITIAN

Today is not good, but tomorrow will come – TSHI

Today is yours, but tomorrow is mine – SURINAMESE

Tomorrow brings many things – TONGA

Tomorrow is pregnant, who knows what it will deliver? – IGBO

You know how much you have passed through; you don't know how much you still have left – HAITIAN

G

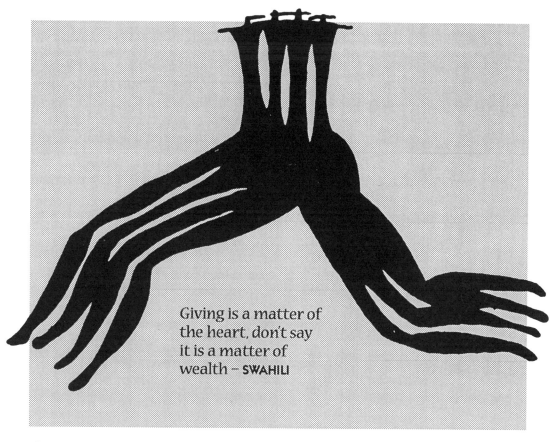

Giving is a matter of the heart, don't say it is a matter of wealth – **SWAHILI**

GAMBLING

Pack ob [of] cards de debil's [devil's] prayer-book – **JAMAICAN**

Before the drawing all lotteries are beautiful – **HAITIAN**

GIFTS & GIVING

Accept if you give – **SWAHILI**

'I don't give you' doesn't mean 'I reject you.' – **MAMPRUSSI**

A little is also a contribution – **IGBO**

As you give so you receive – **UGANDAN**

Better the smallest present than the most magnificent meanness – **HAUSA**

Giving hands receive – **UGANDAN**

Giving is storing up for yourself – **NDEBELE**

Giving to her who has given you something is not giving but paying. Giving to her who does not give you something is not giving, it is throwing away – **SWAHILI**

He who gives to you, stores; he who refuses you, buries – **UGANDAN**

However little a person gives, they is on your side – **UGANDAN**

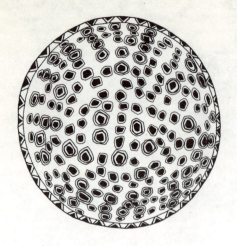

If one gives you little, it's because she lacks much – UGANDAN

One does not love another, if one does not accept anything from her – KANURI / BORNU

One does not usually make a gift with his only possession – IGBO

That which gives is the heart; the fingers only let go – HAYA

To give away is to put away for yourself – TSWANA

To give is to save – OVAMBO

You give to one who gives to you – LUYIA

Give your words with your goods and it will make two gifts – ANCIENT EGYPTIAN

A giver and a receiver, who is more burdened? – SWAHILI

She who asks for nothing will get nothing – HAITIAN

GOD

Even if de [the] devil bring it, God sen'[ds] it – BAJAN

God has only one measure for all people – HAITIAN

God will dry what he has drenched – HAITIAN

If you have forgotten God, you have forgotten yourself – SWAHILI

If you want to speak to God, speak to the winds. [God's omnipresence] – TWI

A person looks only on the outside of things; God looks into the very heart – EFIK

A mortal owns the saying and God owns the fulfilment – MAMPRUSSI

The designs of one's heart do not arrive, but those of God arrive – KIKUYU

The very thing you do not want, that is what pleases God – SWAHILI

The words which men say pass on one side, the things which God does pass on another side – ANCIENT EGYPTIAN

There is but one God for everyone – HAITIAN

What God hath bestowed on you, no-one can take away – HAITIAN

What God sends you, you cannot send back (sickness, death, etc) – GANDA

What is hidden to human beings is plain before God – YORUBA

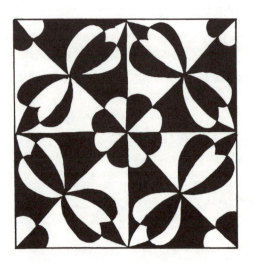

GOODNESS & GOOD NATURE

A good-humoured person has no enemy – IGBO

A white cloth and a stain never agree – YORUBA

De man all honey, fly wi' nyam him – JAMAICAN
The man who's all honey, flies will eat him.

Do good an'[d] good wi'[ll] follow you – JAMAICAN

Goodness begets goodness – UGANDAN

Goodness engenders abuse – SWAHILI

Goodness is done by a bad person, evil cannot be done by a good person – SWAHILI

Hate bad will not do bad – MAMPRUSSI

In a place where good is done, bad deeds are seen at once – SWAHILI

It is easy to be good if you are not provoked – SWAHILI

It is into the heart that the good looks – ANCIENT EGYPTIAN

Return good for evil – HAUSA

(Sometimes) it's painful to be right – HAITIAN

The man who is too good is a fool – HAITIAN

The well-doer reaps hate – HO

Your goodness is not for yourself but for others – EWE

GOSSIP & RUMOUR

A dirty tongue dirties its owner – UGANDAN

A word whispered in someone's ear is often heard far away – HAITIAN

Eyes, let them see, but as for the mouth - there's the danger – FIPA

I will remain alone rather than have a slanderer for my companion – EFIK

Often the lips observe things before the eyes do – HAITIAN

One who tells you about others will tell others about you – SWAHILI

People do not fight over a rumour – MAASAI

Tales are the food of the ear – IGBO

The person who sits to listen to what is said about others, will hear things that will not please him – SHERBRO

The tongue carries that which is light – TSHI

GRADUALNESS

'Tone [stone] by 'Tone de [the] wall fall –
JAMAICAN

A mouse finishes the hide bite by bite – **KIKUYU**

A tree does not grow bent for thirty years
that one should expect to straighten it in one
– **ASHANTI**

Height is not reached in a hurry – **ZULU**

Little by little one goes far – **TSONGA**

Little by little the bird builds its nest –
LOUISIANA

One day cannot make an elephant rot – **LOZI**

Small showers fill the stream – **HAUSA**

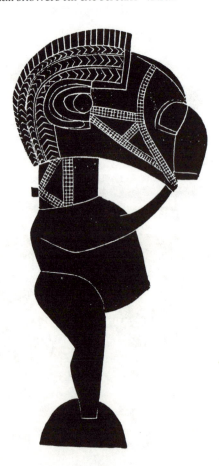

The finger you dip in the pot finishes off the
honey – **UGANDAN**

GRATITUDE

A gift is not despised – **OVAMBO**

Be grateful to the tree so that it may yield
more fruits – **SHONA**

Do not blame God for having created the
tiger, but thank Him for not having given it
wings – **AMHARIC**

Do not break the branch you climbed – **OVAMBO**

Do not despise a bridge on which you have
crossed – **SWAHILI**

Gratitude is not servitude – **SWAHILI**

One who escorts you at night is thanked at
dawn – **BEMBA**

You praise in the morning one who guides
you safely at night – **UGANDAN**

She who receives a gift does not measure –
KIKUYU

How can you like the firewood and dislike the
gatherer? – **UGANDAN**

If you do good to a hundred people and one of
them acknowledges it, no part of it is lost –
ANCIENT EGYPTIAN

One who teaches you how to set a trap: won't
you give her of the meat you catch? – **GANDA**

Remember the rain that made your corn grow – **HAITIAN**

The bush (which shades us) is not to be defiled – **ZULU**

The dog barks more for the person who feeds it than [for] the owner – **OROMO**

The hunter's name is always connected with the meat of the elephant – **TSHI**

The piece of meat cannot be so sweet that you forget the cook who roasted it – **LUYIA**

When a woman's cocoyam is well harvested, she will remember the person who planted it for her – **IGBO**

GREATER & LESSER

A small thing that is thriving is better than a big thing that is ailing – **GANDA**

A town where a wolf kills people in the day time will be terrible at night – **YORUBA**

One who has seen a thousand does not praise a hundred – **TWI**

The woman who is drenched with rain no longer dreads walking through dew – **SHONA**

The person who slaughters a beast does not hesitate about skinning it – **SWAHILI**

If a tortoise wearing a steel coat is burnt to death by fire, what of a fowl with bundles of feathers! – **NIGERIAN**

If big breeze wi' blow 'way anchor, wha' you tink a fowl fedder? – **JAMAICAN**
If a big breeze will blow away an anchor, what do you think will happen to the fowl's feathers?

If one despises a cow, one also despises its strip of hide – **KIKUYU**

If the year doesn't kill you, this day won't kill you – **MAMPRUSSI**

If you lub [love] de cow you mus'[t] lub de calf – **JAMAICAN**

Loose teeth are better than no teeth – **GANDA**

One who eats the egg also eats the chick – **SHONA**

One who pulls a branch along also drags along its leaves – **SHONA**

Sometimes the dregs are to be preferred to the wine – HAITIAN

That which killed the francolin [a pheasant-like bird] breaks the eggs – MAMPRUSSI

The animal that the leopard could not eat, is not eaten by the cat – TSHI

The eye which has seen the king will not fear his officer – HAUSA

Eyes that have beheld the ocean can no longer be afraid of the lagoon – YORUBA

The eyes which have seen the mountains are not moved by valleys – SWAHILI

The hyena said "I am fleet-footed" but the fields said "we are wide." – TSWANA

The owner of a puppy already owns a dog – IGBO

There must be peace in the district to have law and order in the country – OVAMBO

When the tiger is dead, the dog takes [rules] the country – MARTINICAN

Every river that runs into the sea loses its name – TSHI

It is not only giants that do great things – JABO

GREED

A greedy mouse will hear no cat – NAMIBIAN

A tree belonging to an avaricious man bore abundantly; but instead of gathering the fruit little by little, he took an axe and cut it down that he might get all at once – YORUBA

Ant follow fat, fat drown ant – JAMAICAN

Do not drink water in the house of a merchant: he will charge you for it – ANCIENT EGYPTIAN

Don't let what is not yours shine [i.e. appear attractive] in your eyes – UGANDAN

Greedy choke puppy – JAMAICAN

She who wants all, tells the rest to be contented – UGANDAN

If I give you, you take and if I say give me, you take your hand back and run away – TSHI

It's better that you burst rather [than] let good food go to waste – HAITIAN

Lust for gold has turned many a good man into an animal – HAITIAN

Returning a second time led a thief to capture – SWAHILI

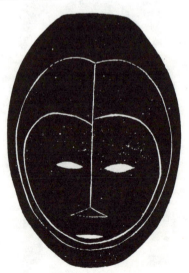

The more one has, the more one wants – **HAITIAN**

You know how to empty but not how to put back – **OVAMBO**

GUESTS

A guest who doesn't eat has come for another reason – **UGANDAN**

Being a guest is a matter of consent – **BONDEI**

If you hear 'welcome,' you will also hear 'May you reach home in safety,' (i.e. the guest will not stay forever) – **HAUSA**

If you invite yourself bring your own chair – **SWAHILI**

The frog says that whoever comes to his home should sit as he sits – **NIGERIAN**

The guest does not surpass the host – **EWE**

When you go to someone's town and she kills a chicken for you to eat, it is not her fowl you have eaten, but your own chicken which is at home.[because she will return the visit] – **TSHI**

Where you are a guest, breakfast is not a right – **LUYIA**

Where you are a guest, you should conceal your opinions – **HAYA**

Who comes in without 'May I come in?,' leaves without 'Goodbye.' – **SWAHILI**

GUILT & CONSCIENCE

A murderer is always afraid of a knife – **HAITIAN**

If they are uttering insults and don't mean you, and yet you reply, you have condemned yourself – **TSHI**

Guilt never decays – **SOTHO**

He who has done something in secret, and sees people talking together, thinks they are talking of his action – **YORUBA**

He who is caught with the hide is the thief – **SWAHILI**

The hyena hides during the day because it knows what it did during the night – OROMO

The tree falls on the person who is there – KIKUYU

The witch suspects everybody of witchcraft – UGANDAN

If an elder were to follow up every offence in order to inflict punishment, the country would go to ruin – TSHI

It is better to be guilty with people than to be guilty with God – MALAGASY

It's because the rat knows what he does at night that he doesn't go out during the day – HAITIAN

No one is sure whether the accused person will accept his guilt – IGBO

The day the old woman disappears is when the hyena excretes grey hair – LOZI

The hand which went into the hole was the one which the scorpion stung – IDOMA

To plead guilty is not to make up for the wrong – SHONA

The head that disturbs the wasps should receive the stings – IGBO

A clear conscience is a soft mat – SWAHILI

Clear conscience sleep a tunda [thunder] – JAMAICAN

The conscience is a compass – SWAHILI

H

One who fetches water at the same place on the riverbank too often ends up in the crocodile – AFRICAN

HABIT

As anything which one is in the habit of doing is natural to them, so a lie is natural to a liar – YORUBA

Habit is a full-grown mountain, hard to get over or to pull down – KONGO

Tr[e]ading on the road constantly makes it smooth – LUO

When water remains too long in a bottle, it stinks – TSHI

With (proper) habits everything is possible – HAITIAN

For a person accustomed to taking, giving away is a battle – SWAHILI

He who dips his fingers in honey, does not do it only once – SWAHILI

HAPPINESS & UNHAPPINESS

As happy as the thief who finds the door left open – HAUSA

Being happy in life is better than being a king – HAUSA

Happiness is the greatest doctor in the world – HAITIAN

Happiness requires something to do, something to love and something to hope for – SWAHILI

If a man is unhappy, his conduct is the cause – TSHI

The fault of happiness is its finishing – HAUSA

Honey is not tasted once – GUSII

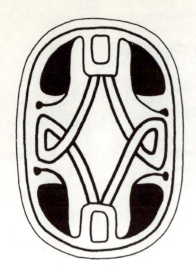

The place where you are happy is better than the place [where] you were born – TSHI

What makes you happy is what will make you sad – HAITIAN

Pleasure's fault is finishing – HAUSA

She who sows joy harvests pleasure – HAITIAN

The place of joy is better than the place [where] one was born – TSHI

To where the heart has rejoiced at night, one returns in the morning – HAYA

Wine, women and food give gladness to the heart – ANCIENT EGYPTIAN

HASTE & DELAY

'Hurry' and 'well' [done] never go hand in hand – HAITIAN

'Too-much-hurry' get dey to-morra, 'tek-time' get dey today – JAMAICAN
Too-much-hurry' gets there tomorrow, 'take-time' gets there today.

Being in a big hurry doesn't mean you know how to get there – HAITIAN

Climbing in haste, falling in haste – SWAHILI

He who takes his food in a hurry, is also choked in a hurry – KIKUYU

Hurry, hurry, get deh [there] tomorrow; tek [take] time, get deh today – CREOLE (BELIZE)

Long road draw sweat, short cut draw blood – JAMAICAN

Quick loving a woman means quick not loving a woman – YORUBA

Better delay and get there – SWAHILI

Delay is the destruction of work – HAUSA

Take a long way and arrive – SWAHILI

'One dese times' nebber done – JAMAICAN
One of these times' is never done.

By the side of 'I shall do' was found 'Not yet done.' – KIKUYU

Better the small deed of the quick than the large one of him who delays – ANCIENT EGYPTIAN

She who says 'now,' is not answered, 'an hour' – SWAHILI

What ripens quickly, rots quickly – GANDA

HATRED

Hate people, but don't give them baskets to fetch water in – TRINIDADIAN

Hate burns its preserver – SWAHILI

Hate has no medicine – GA

It is better to be hated by the king than by the people – MALAGASY

The medicine for hate is separation – FULFULDE

The person who hates you will not lack faults to find in you – SWAHILI

Do not hate someone to their face when you know nothing of them – ANCIENT EGYPTIAN

HEALTH

A healthy young woman climbs mountains – SWAHILI

Health has no price – SWAHILI

Health owns laughter – MAMPRUSSI

For a rash to heal you must stop scratching it – SUKUMA

She who survives two illnesses must have the right medicine – UGANDAN

Medicine does not work where there is no wound – SHONA

The doctor can't drink the medicine for the patient – TSHI

There is no medicine as active as good food – IGBO

You are begging for medicine from a sick person – LAMBA

An abscess heals when opened – THONGA

Birth is the remedy for death – HAUSA

Do not scorn a remedy that you can use – ANCIENT EGYPTIAN

Serious diseases require great remedies – HAITIAN

They have cured my swollen testicles, but they have also cut them off! – UGANDAN

THE HEART

A grove of trees in one's heart cannot be cleared by others – KIKUYU

A man's face shows what is in his heart – HAUSA

A person's heart brings about trouble and solves trouble – MAMPRUSSI

Far from the eyes, far from the heart – HAITIAN

If you want to hear news of the heart ask the face – FULANI

It is better for the eyes to die than the heart – SWAHILI

It is the heart that carries one to hell or to heaven – KANURI

It is the heart that knows – LAMBA

Lip kiss no touch de [the] heart – JAMAICAN

Mothers make children, but not children's hearts – TRINIDADIAN

The body decays, the heart remains – TSONGA

The heart forgets what the eyes do not see – HAITIAN

The mouth talks plenty that the heart does not say – EWE

The thief is the heart, the fingers do not steal – LAMBA

What is stored in the heart does not rot – UGANDAN

What the heart desires is like medicine to it – SWAHILI

What the heart is full of, the mouth speaks of – GANDA

Where the heart desires, there it goes – NYIKA

You shake man'[s] han'[d], you no shake him heart – BAHAMIAN

HEAVEN & HELL

A no eberyting come from heaven a blessin' – JAMAICAN
Not everything that comes from heaven is a blessing.

A sumptuous funeral doesn't mean you're going to heaven – HAITIAN

Betta fe go a Heaven a pauper, dan to Hell a Rectar – JAMAICAN
Better to go to Heaven a pauper, than to hell a Rector.

HELP

A finished knife is the one that is used to make others – LUVALE

Ask help from the spirits after having used all your strength – UGANDAN

Everybody gives advice to build a house, but nobody wants to carry one load of grass – OROMO

Ferry me across shallow waters and I shall ferry you through deeper waters – **LUYIA**

Fire cannot cross a river without an ally – **YORUBA**

She who helps you in need is a friend – **SWAHILI**

Help me during the floods, I will help you during the drought – **HAYA**

Help those who cannot help themselves – **KONGO**

If one does not have another person, [one] cannot get the elephant – **OROMO**

If you have no teeth you will have to persuade others to bite for you – **TSWANA**

Not to aid one in distress is to kill her in your heart – **YORUBA**

One only seeks a guide when one has lost the road – **HAUSA**

One who encounters problems in a crowd will be helped – **KAONDE**

One who has called for help has surrendered – **SHONA**

One who helps you must be stronger than you – **UGANDAN**

The help you give others will soon be your own help – **EWE**

The woman who kills the snake for you is your neighbour – **SUKUMA**

The one who helps is better than the one who laughs – **SWAHILI**

The one who makes an effort is the one who merits help – **KIKUYU**

When the load fatigues the head, the shoulder takes over – **IGBO**

HOME

A small house all your own is always big enough – **HAITIAN**

A wren is a queen in her own nest – **IGBO**

Dry bread in one's home is better than good meat somewhere else – **SWAHILI**

Everyone knows what is boiling in her own pot – **HAITIAN**

He who dies far from his town, is buried only out of pity – **ANCIENT EGYPTIAN**

Hit [it] take two birds fer [for] to make a nest – AFRICAN-AMERICAN

Home is where you are content – SWAHILI

It is not the fire in the fireplace which warms the house, but the couple who get along well – MALAGASY

Not where I was born, but where it goes well with me is my home – KANURI

People are the home – AFRICAN

The horse never refuses a homeward gallop – YORUBA

The house is for sleeping in by night, not for staying in by day – KIKUYU

When a nation is declining, it begins in its homes – TSHI

HONESTY

De hones' man nod betta dan de rogue' bond – JAMAICAN
The honest man's nod is better than the rogue's bond.

Too long honest, too long poor – BAJAN

She who doesn't say it to you isn't your friend – NDONGA

If your child is dancing clumsily, tell him: 'you are dancing clumsily'; do not tell him: 'darling, do as you please.' – TWI

A straight road has no turnings – EFIK

The remedy for 'don't let it be heard' is 'don't let it be done' – HAUSA

Who pays his tax has nothing to fear – TSONGA

HONOUR & DISHONOUR

Hell itself holds dishonour in horror – TAMASHEK

Honour does not come by itself, it must be brought in – SWAHILI

If you are honoured, honour yourself – TWI

Honour a child and it will honour you – ILA

The one who took the pains and headaches now deserves the honour – HAITIAN

HOPE

As long as your head is not cut off, there is still hope for you – HAITIAN

 **H**

Don't give up hope until you fill in the grave
– UGANDAN

Fire devours the grass, but not the roots –
EWE

Hope is the pillar of the world – KANURI

Hope kills nobody – KONGO

What one hopes for is better than what one
finds – GALLA

HUMANITY/HUMAN NATURE

A baboon is a human being: it knows the
art of clandestine stealing – SHONA

A chief reigns over hyenas and crocodiles as
well as over useful animals – TSONGA

A human being, unlike a country, cannot be
thoroughly known – TSWANA

A man is a man, and a dog is a dog – LAMBA

A witch is human: when pricked he cries –
SHONA

As there is guilt in innocence, there is
innocence in guilt – YORUBA

Deceit is not a thing of yesterday only –
GANDA

Domestic animals can be enslaved; a
human being will free herself – SHONA

Even a fool is a human being – OVAMBO

Even a poor man has a heart – TSWANA

Even if a witch's child dies, it makes her sad
– TSHI

God loves him who cares for the poor, more
than him who respects the wealthy –
ANCIENT EGYPTIAN

He who inflicts punishment does not forbid
crying – EWE

If you were medicine you would be very
bitter – EFIK

In order to find evil doers, every human
being is given a name – TSHI

In the midst of your illness you will promise
a goat, but when you have recovered, a
chicken will seem sufficient – JUKUN

Languages differ but coughs are the same –
NIGERIAN

H

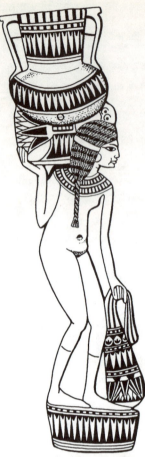

People are the thing: if I call 'Gold,' gold does not respond; if I call 'Clothes,' clothes do not respond; people are the thing – TWI

Slippery ground does not recognise kings – LUYIA

Smoke rises from beneath every roof – BAMBARA

Tall and short teeth all eat the same way – TSHI

There is no foot which does not stumble – ZULU

Wealth is a matter of the heart – SWAHILI

Wha'[t] got blood got feelin.' – BAJAN

When man say him no mine, den him mine – JAMAICAN
When a man says he doesn't mind, then he minds.

When you see an old bone on the highway, remember that once it was covered with flesh – HAITIAN

Where there is nothing to lose there is nothing to fear – SWAHILI

Youth is hope, old age is remembrance – SWAHILI

HUMOUR

Jesting brings forth quarrels, quarrels deprive of control over words – SWAHILI

There is truth even in humour – OVAMBO

Laughter is the same anywhere in the world – YORUBA

There is laughter in spite of bitterness in the heart – OVAMBO

Everyone can be witty, but good sense is rare – HAITIAN

HUNGER

A hungry man is an angry man – IGBO

A hungry person has no mind for any other matter – NIGERIAN

A hungry stomach knows no law – TSONGA

Hunger chases away the soul and brings in madness – UGANDAN

Hunger does not reason – HAITIAN

Hunger doesn't seek good food – UGANDAN

Hunger is the remedy for poor cooking – HAUSA

Hunger will make a monkey eat pepper – HAITIAN

Hunger will make dogs climb caymite trees – HAITIAN

Hungry belly man na [doesn't] know soup na [isn't] sweet – GUYANAN

Poor food does not kill as many as starvation – TSHI

Sweetness does not satisfy hunger – KIKUYU

The belly orders the work – TSONGA

What hunger wants is satisfaction – TSHI

Once one is beset by hunger, thoughtfulness will disappear – YORUBA

He who is fatter starves more during famine – UGANDAN

'If' does not fill the larder – OVAMBO

If you are merciful to the antelope, you go to bed hungry – TSHI

You plan to overcome hunger in two days, but it kills in one day – UGANDAN

HUNTING

A dogless hunter must crawl in the hole himself – OVAMBO

A hunter is not afraid of thorns – SWAHILI

An elephant hunter usually gets killed by an elephant – SWAHILI

It's useless for the elephant to be huge since the hunter kills it – MAMPRUSSI

To the hunter the animal that gets away is always a big one – TSHI

Nobody makes a rope in front of an animal he hopes to catch – TSHI

The person who runs in a thorn-infested forest is either running after something or something is running after him – YORUBA

HYPOCRISY

Blind man see him neighbour fault – JAMAICAN

'Don't give' likes 'get.' – MAMPRUSSI

A twister (double-dealer) is a man who invites you to a meal and talks about your voracity afterwards – GANDA

He who finds others' food sweet, finds it bitter when others come to his house – UGANDAN

One who promises to forget is the one who hopes to remember – HAITIAN

His mouth is sweet, but his heart is full of hatred – MALAGASY

If you give it to the monkey, the monkey accepts it; if you ask from the monkey, the monkey says 'No.' – TWI

Na all daag wah play wid you gat you good a-he min' – GUYANAN
Not all dogs that play with you have your good in mind.

Sometimes white face carry black haat [heart] – GUYANAN

The well-fed calls the ravenous greedy – KIKUYU

Throw the stone, hide your hand – HAITIAN

To the white horse the zebra said: 'I am white too' and to the black horse: 'I am really black.' – NAMIBIAN

What I do to others I do not like others to do to me – SWAHILI

While he deprecates the quality of [the] food, he eats a lot of it – GURAGE

You run away from a crocodile but eat crocodile stew – JUKUN

Anger in the mind, smile on the teeth – IGBO

Before face an'[d] behin'[d] back no a one – JAMAICAN
Before the face and behind the back isn't the same.

Behind darg [dog] it is, 'Darg,' before darg it is, 'Mr Darg.' – JAMAICAN

Daag deh, "Mr Daag"; daag no deh no mo': "Daag." – GUYANAN
Dog there, 'Mr Dog'; dog not there: 'Dog.'

Do not separate your mind from your tongue. – ANCIENT EGYPTIAN

All plants are medicinal, but if you don't know you say some are useless – **TSHI**

IGNORANCE

A child who remains in his mother's house believes her soup the best – **EFIK**

One who never travels thinks it is only his mother who is a good cook – **KIKUYU**

One who has not seen the new moon before, calls the stars the moon – **VAI**

A man who knows nothing does not know that he knows nothing – **GANDA**

A monkey broke the razor after shaving, not knowing that his hair would soon grow again – **NIGERIAN**

A person who rushes to war doesn't know he may meet death – **IGBO**

As the child has not seen what happened before his birth, let [him] be satisfied with having it told him – **EWE**

She who knows nothing doubts nothing – **HAITIAN**

If one doesn't know trees, one treats them all as firewood – **UGANDAN**

Ignorance caused the chicken to sleep hungry on top of the bundle of corn – **HAUSA**

Ignorance is night – **MAMPRUSSI**

It takes a heap of licks to drive a nail in the dark – **AFRICAN-AMERICAN**

Knowing too much is being ignorant – **KIKUYU**

Not to know is bad, not to wish to know is worse – **WOLOF**

The 'apatipere' bird says: 'If one doesn't know, someone teaches him.' – **TSHI**

The herb you trample will cure you – **OVAMBO**

The ignorant praises his own ignorance – **SWAHILI**

The ignorant thirsts [while] sitting by the water-side – **OROMO**

The untutored, the uncomprehending, learn their lessons through public ridicule – **YORUBA**

Wanting the impossible is caused by ignorance – **SWAHILI**

When the music stops a deaf person continues to dance – **IGBO**

When you don't know the leopard, you get eaten – **FIPA**

When you don't know, you carry water in a basket – **HAITIAN**

It's when a person doesn't know that trouble overcomes him – **MAMPRUSSI**

IMAGINATION

Distant fire-wood is good fire-wood – **EWE**

Dreaming comes prior to getting – **MAMPRUSSI**

If you have no eye, then the mind takes you there – **JABO**

It is painful when you dream of the one who has rejected you – **SHONA**

The head which has dreams is superior – **TSHI**

The imagination you have is as far-fetched as that of the bird that migrated at night, imagining it had to pay tax – **GANDA**

The man who watches a wrestling match imagines many ways to defeat an opponent; he knows not the difficulties involved – **IGBO**

The other person's cloth is beautiful – **KAONDE**

The other person's load is always lighter – **HAYA**

You sleep on the road, and dreaming, think you have reached your destination – **MONGO**

IMITATION

Beast follows monkey, it breaks its leg – **IGBO**

Don't copy the elephant in eating thorns – **SWAHILI**

Follow-fashion bruk [broke] monkey neck – **JAMAICAN**

Follow-follow kill monkey – **BAJAN**

Most achievements come about by imitation
– **HAYA**

IMPORTANCE

An eye is small but its usefulness is great –
MAMPRUSSI

She is a large tree on which all things hang,
or are entwined: if she falls, all perish – **EFIK**

When you go to fetch water and do not
return, they do not enquire about the pot – **OJI**

Where an elephant is being killed, none
notices the death of a monkey – **HAUSA**

Where an elephant is dead a hare will not
smell – **FULANI**

IMPOSSIBILITY

A hunchback is never asked to stand upright
– **YORUBA**

A stream coming down won't let you swim up
– **EFIK**

After throwing the spear it is impossible to
catch the tail of it – **OROMO**

If a child burns its belly and the mother
burns her back, carrying becomes impossible
– **SHONA**

No matter how hastily you eat, you don't
swallow your tongue – **FULFULDE**

No, the heavens do not ever come down to
the earth, the hills do not come down to the
valleys – **HAUSA**

One cannot blow the fire with water in his
mouth – **IGBO**

You cannot dodge an arrow at night – **KAONDE**

When coc'[o]nut fall from tree he can't fasten
back – **GUYANAN**

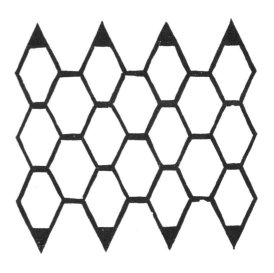

INABILITY

An empty gun cannot fire – **TEMNE**

Broken pitcher can'[t] carry water – **JAMAICAN**

He who is unable to dance says that the yard
is stony – **KIKUYU**

I am not able to carry my load, and yet you
say, 'help me!' – **TSHI**

If a case is greater than your wisdom and you
give an answer to it, you usually don't get the
right solutions to it – **TSHI**

It is in one's mind; but hands are not there to
do it – **IGBO**

Lilly [little] axe can' [can't] cut down big tree –
JAMAICAN

Melons drop down for those without pots –
NDEBELE

The mouse on the path to the waterhole
hears of trouble but won't be able to speak –
MAMPRUSSI

Tortoise wants to knock but its arm is too
short – **SHERBRO**

What is beyond the reach of a tall man will
not be achieved by a short one – **FIPA**

INDIFFERENCE & NEGLECT

A consumer of eggs has no regard for the pain the hen has in laying them – YORUBA

He who neglects the thorn in his foot gets elephantiasis – SWAHILI

If another suffers pain, to you a piece of wood suffers – OJI

In an abandoned house, lizards roam around, multiply and fight – UGANDAN

Pain in your neighbour's body is like pain in a tree – TSHI

The arrow in another's body is as though in the quiver – FULANI

What affects another person is like [something] affecting a log – SHONA

There is no medicine for the sickness that will kill you – TSHI

There is no sea without waves – SWAHILI

Though the cock does not crow, the sun will rise – TSONGA

Though the night tarry, the dawn will break – KONGO

Two buttocks cannot avoid friction – TONGA

Two t'[h]ing a-run, one must win – GUYANAN

When men fight by the light of the moon, the bald ones are sure to be hit – MALAGASY

When the snail moves the shell follows – NIGERIAN

Whenever you shoot a lizard leaning on a tree, you also shoot that tree – MAMPRUSSI

You can't bring light to your neighbour when it is dark at your own home – SWAHILI

You cannot manage horses: how can you cater for elephants? – SWAHILI

You nebber [never] see empty pot bwoil [boil] over – JAMAICAN

INEXPERIENCE

Don't talk of hunger to one who never missed a meal – UGANDAN

One who has had a full meal does not know

the hungry person – **SWAHILI**

The person who has not made the journey calls it an easy one – **GANDA**

He who laughs at a scar has not received a wound – **SWAHILI**

If a child is entrusted with a large amount of money, he will incur big debts – **TSHI**

Inexperience and foolhardiness motivate the mouse to wish to engage the cat in a fight – **YORUBA**

Those who have experienced nothing mistake the sound of weeping for singing – **EWE**

When a child is learning to make designs, she does not practice on a leopard's skin – **TSHI**

INFLUENCE

A bad coconut spoils good ones – **SWAHILI**

A low person makes another person low – **GURAGE**

If you lib wid darg you larn fe howl – **JAMAICAN**
If you live with a dog you learn to howl.

One rotten sheep wi' 'pwoil de whole flock – **JAMAICAN**
One rotten sheep will spoil the whole flock.

Some people are not inherently bad but are made wicked by others – **HAYA**

Those who stay with roses also smell like roses – **SWAHILI**

INGRATITUDE

A person who is given butter will give back a stone – **OROMO**

Do a man a favour and he'll never forgive you – **HAITIAN**

Do not cover a snake under your cloak: when it gets warm it will bite you – **TSWANA**

Han'[d] mek [makes] rope, rope tie han.' – **GUYANAN**

He who has crossed over forgets the ferryman – **GANDA**

He whom you teach to cultivate does not give you anything of what he grows in abundance – **GANDA**

If one who receives help is ungrateful, she gets no help again – **IGBO**

If you bring up a dog with milk, it will bite you first thing tomorrow – **SHONA**

People count the refusals, [they] do not count the gifts – KIKUYU

The gratitude that bees receive (for their diligent work in collecting honey) is the smoke that people use to expel them and get at their honey – SWAHILI

The needy begs, but once his needs are satisfied he forgets quickly those he begged from – HAYA

The one who has helped others climb the ladder, gets kicked in the teeth – SWAHILI

The ox rewards with kicks – CHAGGA

The peace-maker receives blows – TSHI

The ungrateful harden the hearts of the generous – UGANDAN

The wheat hates the rain that made it grow – GURAGE

They like her gifts but dislike her – HAYA

When you take a squirrel out of the water, it contrives a plot against you – DUALA

Whenever you heal the monkey's missing tooth, he uses it to nibble at your corn – MAMPRUSSI

You have cured his testicles, and he has used them on your wife – UGANDAN

The eyes which you cure will one day look at you with envy – LUO

INJURY

A delicate thing is not difficult to injure – YORUBA

A man who has done evil to you makes you hate all men – GANDA

A scar is easily wounded – SWAHILI

He that did it forgets; she who suffered it does not – SOTHO

She who hurts another hurts also herself – UGANDAN

It is not difficult to hurt, but it is difficult to repair – TSONGA

Not all wounds heal – HAITIAN

People who hurt you will never forgive you – HAITIAN

The axe forgets, the tree doesn't forget – NDEBELE

The offended one does not forget, the offender forgets – OVAMBO

INNOCENCE

I have made no one to weep – ANCIENT EGYPTIAN

Pepper which you have not eaten: how does it burn you? – SWAHILI

The person who stays indoors cannot be accused of what happens outside – YORUBA

To be told, 'You stink,' does not affect the clean – UGANDAN

The composure of the one who does no wrong isn't disturbed – MAMPRUSSI

You are blaming the hawk, [while] the falcon is killing the chickens – SWAHILI

INSIGHT & UNDERSTANDING

I dislike those who quickly understand my limits and virtues – UGANDAN

If thou knowest a man's character thou mayest safely live with him – HAUSA

Man know you' face, but he na know you' haat – GUYANAN
A man knows your face, but he doesn't know your heart.

The heart's eye sees many things – SWAHILI

He who is spoken to at both ears does not understand – KIKUYU

She who says: "I didn't understand," is not stupid – SWAHILI

It is not the eye that understands, but the mind – HAUSA

Seeing something does not mean that you know it – TSONGA

The one who listens is the one who understands – JABO

Pick sense out a [of] nonsense – CREOLE (BELIZE)

The ability to see shows a person the way – KIKUYU

Looking carefully is understanding – OVAMBO

Too great eagerness bereaves [one] of understanding – SWAHILI

INSIGNIFICANCE

A little splinter despised can make you limp – UGANDAN

A little, contemptible path is sometimes the one that leads you to the highway – KIKUYU

A small thing is not noticed in a crowd – ILA

I

Even if many mice dig a hole, it doesn't become deep – **TSHI**

Even that which is despised could triumph – **MAASAI**

Nothin'[g] fuh [for] nothin' an very little fuh somethin'[g] – **BAJAN**

Sorry fe [for] poor t[h]ing, poor ting kill you – **JAMAICAN**

String added to string will bind even a leopard – **OJI**

The forest you overlook is the place the rope will come from to tie you up – **AFRICAN**

The tree on which we lean and which cannot support us, if it falls down on us it cannot kill us – **YORUBA**

You are fighting over the difference between seven and six – **SUKUMA**

INSULT

A big insult, a hard knock – **EWE**

A man will not publicly insult me and then apologise privately – **HAUSA**

She who insults you does not choose her insults for you (i.e. she does not mince her words) – **SWAHILI**

If you laugh at the bowl, you laugh at the potter (its maker) – **GANDA**

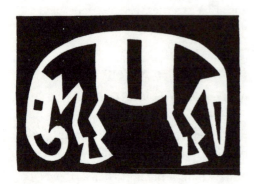

If you sneer at an impudent person, you have to worry about what he (she) will answer – **GANDA**

INTEREST

'A message is no load': so you say if you like the place you are being sent to – **GANDA**

A bald-headed man does not care for a razor – **YORUBA**

A child doesn't forget where she received a gift – **SUKUMA**

A dog does not leave the place where it picked a bone – **LUYIA**

A hungry person is never sent to the granary
– LUYIA

It is the owner of the farm who drives off a
leopard, not someone else – HAUSA

Only those who have teeth worry about
toothache – GBANDE

The woman kidnapped where she longs to be
married, tells her people to delay [taking]
action – IGBO

Where yours is, there the way is not long –
OVAMBO

INTIMACY

If trouses say massa tief, you can't paca
(doubt) – GUYANAN
If the trousers say their master is a thief, you can't doubt.

It is the woman that knows the man that
calls another 'small penis.' – IGBO

Shoe know if stockin'[g] hab [have] hole –
BAHAMIAN

To stay together is to know each other –
KIKUYU

Let me sleep a night in the room and I shall
know the hole in the roof – SWAHILI

If you have no child, you will not give advice
about children – JABO

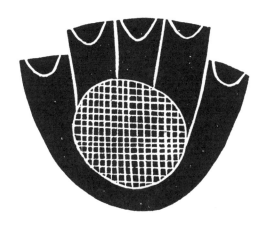

INVOLVEMENT

Both she that chases and she that is chased
become tired – KIKUYU

He who comes between two brothers when
they quarrel will be placed between them
when they are reconciled – ANCIENT EGYPTIAN

If anything touches the nose the eye waters –
HAUSA

If green leaves burn, what of dry ones? – TEMNE

If one finger is hurt, the other fingers are
bleeding – SWAHILI

If you don't go to a place, you don't ask for the
path to it – MAMPRUSSI

If you no wan' leaf drop 'pon you, 'tan' from
under de tree – JAMAICAN
If you don't want the leaf to drop upon you, stand from under the
tree.

One burning house burns the next – UGANDAN

One intervenes only in matters referred to one – YORUBA

One who throws mud gets himself soiled as well – SWAHILI

Play with the cat, and you'll get scratched – MARTINIQUE

The breeze that knocks down [the] green trees will not leave the dry – TEMNE

The chased and the one who chases get tired – KIKUYU

The foot that travels the road [is] the one that is pricked by the thorn – JABO

'The heavens will fall' is not the concern of only one individual – YORUBA

The one who holds the pan is the one who feels the heat – HAITIAN

The pot will smell of that which is put into it – SWAHILI

The thief does not gossip about his accomplice – JABO

The vine does not laugh at a burning tree – EWE

Water only drowns the swimmer – UGANDAN

What is hidden is known by the one who hid it – HAYA

When one finger [is] soil[ed] with oil, it will extend to other fingers – IGBO

When the leg breaks, the eye sheds tears – SHONA

When two daag get quarrel, Tom cat 'tan' wan side – GUYANAN
When two dogs quarrel, the cat stands to one side.

Who play wid [with] de puppy get bit wid de fleas – GUYANAN

You play wid tar mus'[t] black you finger – JAMAICAN

The neighbour's water is never muddy; it is always clean – **YORUBA**

JEALOUSY & ENVY

A stone will sooner soften than jealousy – **TSWANA**

If a person has, don't let it worry you – **MAMPRUSSI**

If jealousy caused hunger, then all people would be hungry – **TSHI**

One's getting pains another – **MAMPRUSSI**

God made the silk-cotton tree beautiful, so let the fig-tree cease being angry – **HAUSA**

The star says, kill the moon for me so that I can shine like the moon – **IGBO**

JUDGEMENT

A child takes a morsel to others of the same size [as] she can put into her own mouth – **GURAGE**

A man of sound judgement cannot be deceived – TSONGA

Do not praise your work in the field, when they (i.e. the visitors) see it with their own eyes – GANDA

Go alone, you are judged by God; go with another, you are judged by people – MALAGASY

It is not all rivers that you bathe in – TSHI

Judgement must wait to hear all the witnesses – IGBO

Judging is judging oneself – SWAHILI

One who has seen a hundred does not praise twenty – TSHI

The chicken left the person who killed it and took its anger out on the pot – IGBO

The eye does not choose the best – MAASAI

What one states in a case [one] is judged by – IGBO

JUSTICE & INJUSTICE

She is as undecided as an orphan: if she does not wash her hands, she will be told she is a dirty child; if she washes his hands, she will be told she is wasting water – MALAGASY

It's always a double punishment to beat a child and ask her not to cry – IGBO

Justice becomes injustice when it makes two wounds on a head which only deserves one – KONGO

The corn is never declared innocent in the court of chickens – EWE

The labourer is always in the sun; the landowner is always in the shade – YORUBA

The peacemaker dies, while the fighters survive – UGANDAN

K

Those who destroy the body are not destroyers of the soul – **SWAHILI**

KILLING

A little prisoner (led away to be killed) who is obstreperous brings the killing place much nearer [i.e. he will be killed on the spot.] – **GANDA**

Human blood is heavy, and hinders the one who has shed it from fleeing – **SOTHO**

When they want to kill a dog, they say it's mad – **HAITIAN**

You have a share in it, but I will not give it to you: this made the proud person commit murder – **TSHI**

KINDNESS

A big heart is better than a big brain – **SWAHILI**

Anticipate kindness from the happy person – **HAUSA**

Be kind to one who is kind to you – **MONGO**

Kindness is better than wealth – **UGANDAN**

Kindness is never lost – **KONGO**

One who is good to others is best to herself – **NIGERIAN**

The reward of benevolence is gratitude – **TSHI**

Too much kindness made a man lend his door – **UGANDAN**

If a person confers a benefit upon another, that benefit is not lost – **KANURI / BORNU**

The only friendly cow is the one which gives milk – **KIKUYU**

Generosity doesn't need compulsion – **UGANDAN**

If you see a man in a gown eating with one in rags, the food belongs to the latter – **FULANI**

No matter how generous you are, you don't give your wife away – **TSHI**

KNOWLEDGE & KNOWING

A hunter has no mysterious notions about the forest – **SHONA**

A little knowledge is no use – **ANGASS**

An uninitiated person is a child – **KURIA**

Early knowledge is better than 'had I known.' – **MAMPRUSSI**

The one who goes in front knows the way – **UGANDAN**

K

If a fish comes out of the water, and says the crocodile has one eye, who will deny? – IGBO

If you do not know where you come from, you must know where you are going to – EWE

If you follow wha' riber carry, you neber drink de water – JAMAICAN
If you follow [consider] what the river carries, you'll never drink the water.

If you knew where bees go, you wouldn't eat honey – SUKUMA

If you know about a knife, the knife won't cut you again – MAMPRUSSI

If you know the beginning well, the end will not trouble you – WOLOF

If you pay attention to what chickens eat, you will never wish to eat chicken – LUYIA

If your grandfather informs you of trouble, you shouldn't ask your father – MAMPRUSSI

It is the eye that has seen the smoke that will perceive the fire – HAUSA

Knowing everything doesn't (necessarily) make you intelligent – HAITIAN

Knowing too much is like being ignorant – KIKUYU

Knowledge is better than riches – EFIK

Knowledge is like a baobab tree (monkey-bread tree) and no one person can embrace it with both arms – EWE

Knowledge is power – KIKUYU

Knowledge kept to oneself is as useless as a candle burning in a pot – OROMO

Man mus' pay fo' larn sense – GUYANAN
Man must pay to learn sense.

Nebber buy puss in a bag – JAMAICAN
Never buy a cat in a bag.

Repeat only a matter seen, not what is heard – ANCIENT EGYPTIAN

Say, 'That's a good place to eat,' when you have been there – UGANDAN

Someone who knows overpowers the one who doesn't know – MAMPRUSSI

That which the ear has heard, and the eye has seen, it is useless for your mouth to deny – MONGO

The eye does not buy a rag – VAI

The hoe is bought after being seen – ZULU

The one who asks the way does not get lost – AFRICAN

To know too much may confuse – KIKUYU

When eye no see mout'[h] no talk – BAHAMIAN

You are never late if you know where you are going – UGANDAN

If you care about what poultry eats you cannot eat chicken – LUYIA

If one person does not know, another explains – ASHANTI

L

If a tree doesn't have branches it doesn't have shade – **SUKUMA**

If firewood is lacking, the fire dies – **SWAHILI**

If one has not got many dresses, one cannot consider any dress as old-fashioned – **YORUBA**

Needle may mek [make] clothes, but him naked himself – **JAMAICAN**

The needle says that he is among bales of cloth but he is still naked – **EWE**

Nothing can suffice a person except that which thet have not – **AFRICAN-AMERICAN**

Same day man get good soup him can'[t] get good foo-foo [porridge] – **JAMAICAN**

The wife of the potter eats from a potsherd – **UGANDAN**

The woman with cloth has no child while the one with a child has no cloth – **KORANKO**

There is no fire when there is no wood – **OVAMBO**

Too much o' nutten ent good – **BAJAN**
Too much of nothing isn't good.

LACK

A stick that is out of reach cannot help you in your fight – **TSONGA**

An empty hand does not go to market – **EWE**

An ironsmith never has a knife – **TSWANA**

Dem short fe singer when dem put peacock a choir – **JAMAICAN**
They are short of a singer when they put the peacock in the choir

Who ha'[s] finger nail no ha'[ve] itch, and who ha itch no ha finger [nail] – **JAMAICAN**

De want of a ting is more dan de wort' – **JAMAICAN**
The want of a thing is more than the worth.

One cut won't bring down a tree – **HAUSA**

To run in the company of one carrying water is no remedy for dirt – **HAUSA**

LAZINESS

A man who says, 'A master does not carry loads,' becomes lazy – GANDA

A lazy person does not know they are lazy until they drive a tortoise away and it escapes – HAUSA

A lazy person looks for light employment – YORUBA

A lazy worker blames the tools – KIKUYU

De [the] lazy jackass can't carry he [his] own oats – GUYANAN

He wants to eat but not work – OVAMBO

If you sleep, your business will sleep too – SWAHILI

Laziness and hunger are twins – SWAHILI

Lazy at work while active at eating – HAYA

Lazy people like to eat everything already cooked – HAITIAN

Sitting together won't do the work – MAMPRUSSI

Sweating when he eats, cold when he works – OVAMBO

The heart of a lazy person desires and has nothing – IGBO

The idler eats his idleness – NDEBELE

The lazy are always the most tired – MALAGASY

The lazy one does not build – OVAMBO

"The lazy person who goes to borrow a spade says, "I hope I won't find one!" – MALAGASY

The mole digs the hole, and another animal enters and dwells in it – UGANDAN

The water flows in the river, the people are thirsty at home – OROMO

When you sleep, your business, too, will sleep – SWAHILI

You are as lazy as a fish: it lives in the water and needs not wash itself to be clean – GANDA

You are only thirsty when somebody has drawn the water – KIKUYU

You did not appear at work-time, but you are visible at food-time – NAMIBIAN

Sleep on, we shall do the hoeing, you just do the eating! – LAMBA

A load of salt on another man's head is easily carried – KONGO

The lazy person's 'tomorrow' will not finish and his 'years' never end – OROMO

The millet of the person who 'would have' used the catapult [to kill birds], is eaten (by birds) – SWAHILI

LEADERS & LEADERSHIP

Although the horse is stupid, it does not follow that the rider is stupid – TSHI

Bad paster [pastor] mek [make] sheep shabby – JAMAICAN

Blind hoss [horse] don't fall w[h]en he follers [follows] de [the] bit – AFRICAN-AMERICAN

Cattle or goats which have no herder graze in others' fields – SWAHILI

One who runs slowly is not made to go first – OVAMBO

If there is no head, the tail will not act – IGBO

The feet go the way of the head – TSHI

The goats, having a lame leader, do not arrive at the grass – KIKUYU

The one who is nearest the enemy, in pursuit, is the real leader – GANDA

The thread always follows the needle – EWE

When the leaders are wise, so are the people – MALAGASY

When you have caught the mother hen, you pick up the chicks without difficulty – ASHANTI

Where there is a herd without a bull, a castrated ox will rule – BORAN

Where the front leg of a cow steps, the hind legs step too – KIPSIGIS

A blind person does not show another the way – KIKUYU

In a village of the blind, the one-eyed man is chief – MAMPRUSSI

The blind person doesn't control the leader – MAMPRUSSI

Follow where the water goes – SWAHILI

If the chief does not stay to fight, the slave runs away – TSHI

The tail must follow the head – KRU

LIABILITY

A dog that bites strangers today may bite its masters tomorrow – SHONA

A man with a beard shouldn't blow on fire – IGBO

Animals with long tails don't jump over the fire – HAITIAN

De same knife dat cut goat t[h]roat can cut sheep troat – JAMAICAN

He who puts on a white dress does not sit near a palm oil seller – NIGERIAN

If a snake bites your neighbour, you too are in danger – SWAHILI

If sentence is now passed on your neighbour, another time it will be passed on you – OJI

If the mouse gnaws stones, then the melon is frightened – EWE

Man dey carry 'traw musn't fool wid fire – JAMAICAN
The man who carries straw mustn't fool with fire.

Same knife weh [that] stick [stabs] sheep stick goat – CREOLE (BELIZE)

The firewood that is about to burn does not laugh at the one already burning – KAMBA

The foot that travels the road is the one that is pricked by the thorn – JABO

What enters amongst the goats [i.e. a predator] will enter amongst the sheep – FULANI

What has befallen me today will befall you tomorrow – SHONA

When a fowl eats your neighbour's corn, drive it away; another time it will eat yours – OJI

When a stone hangs in the air, the pot is afraid – NIGERIAN

When the turkey is being plucked, the hen doesn't laugh – HAITIAN

Wood already touched by fire is not hard to start burning again – TSHI

LIES & DECEPTION

A lie is a child's way of escaping (punishment) – GANDA

False accusation pains more than a machete wound – IGBO

If you know how to tell lies, do you know how to run away? – TSHI

If you sow falsehood, you reap deceit – AFRICAN

Liars should have good memories – SWAHILI

Lies return – KAONDE

Mr 'I-Was-There' is the only one who may tame a lie – UGANDAN

One lie destroys a thousand truths – TWI

The person who travels without a companion tells lies – TSHI

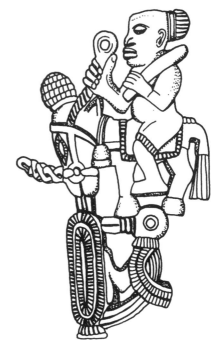

Whoever does not lie does not stay alive – OVAMBO

Whoever trades in lies will pay in truth – HAUSA

De [the] same trick don'[t] serve a person twice – BAJAN

Fool me once, shame on you; fool me twice, shame on me – BAJAN

I would rather be deceived by an intelligent person than by a jackass – HAITIAN

The eye usually deceives itself – KAMBA

There is no one who is clever when she is cheated – MAASAI

LIFE

A living dog is better than a dead lion – IGBO

Arriving and leaving, hoping and remembering, that's what life consists of – HAITIAN

L

Life is a slow journey towards death – HAITIAN

One who is serious all day will never have a good time, while one who is frivolous all day will never establish a household – ANCIENT EGYPTIAN

The depth of a person's life is more important than its length – SWAHILI

There are things in life that we must accept – HAITIAN

There are three things worth having in this world: courage, good sense, and caution – HAUSA

There is no difference between growing old and living – KIKUYU

You only have a short time to live; make good use of your time – HAITIAN

LIKE & DISLIKE

He who dislikes you dislikes whatever belongs to you – TWI

If a person doesn't like you, she doesn't like anything about you – TSHI

If you like daag, you mus' like 'e tail – GUYANAN
If you like the dog, you must also like his tail.

That which is making your mouth sick will not prevent your friends from eating – SUKUMA

The remedy for dislike is separation – HAUSA

What one person eats, that another one detests – IGBO

What a woman likes she does – TSHI

A cry-baby won't be rescued from red ants – UGANDAN

As long as we are alive, there are still many achievements before us – YORUBA

Cry for life, don't cry for money – TSHI

De longer yuh [you] live, de more yuh hear – BAJAN

Disappointment is not difficult and happiness is not difficult – JABO

Life can be understood backwards but we live it forwards – SWAHILI

Life has only one door, death has a hundred – HAITIAN

LIKENESS

A dog does not steal from another dog – TEMNE

A partridge gives birth to another partridge – TSONGA

A snake is like a rope, but it is not (for that reason) taken to bind a thing with – ASHANTI

Alligator lay egg but him no fowl – JAMAICAN

Anyone with an anus will not laugh at another's fart – OVAMBO

Everybody likes those like [themselves] – WOLOF

Fire doesn't put out fire – SUKUMA

He who sees one, sees all, because they are all alike – TSONGA

If the vulture speaks to the wolf, he listens – TWI

Ill attracts ill – RUANDA

It is a thief that can trace the footsteps of another thief on a rock – YORUBA

One who does not behave like a monkey cannot catch a monkey alive – YORUBA

One who does not know what darkness is like is advised to shut his eyes – IGBO

Similar characters make a friendship – YORUBA

Sleep and being killed: there is not a long distance between them – AFRICAN

Two people who are in exactly the same position should have no cause to criticize one another – HAYA

What is in the house of the wasp is also in the house of the bee – IGBO

What you like in a book is you yourself – HAITIAN

When a mad man speaks, a mad man understands him – KORANKO

Who no know dead, leh 'e look 'pon sleep – GUYANAN
Who doesn't know death, let him look upon sleep.

You are not the crocodile's brother, though you swim well by his side – MENDE

LIMITATION

A child able to run doesn't know how to hide
– MAMPRUSSI

A fruit can'[t] fall no further dan [than] de
tree – BAJAN

One can only do some of the things to be
done in the world and not all – TWI

A person scratches herself where her hand
can reach – SWAHILI

A short man can only hang his bag on that
part of the wall he is able to reach – IGBO

Darg hab four foot, but him can' walk four
different pass (ways) – JAMAICAN
The dog has four feet, but he can't walk along four different
roads.

Ebery man hang him bonkra (hand-basket)
wha' him han' can ketch – JAMAICAN
Every man hangs his hand-basket where his hand can catch [i.e.
reach].

God knew how the snake is and made it
without legs – OROMO

Great ideas and small capability – HAITIAN

He knows how to run, (but) he doesn't know
how to hide – HAITIAN

Muzzle darg no ketch rat – JAMAICAN
The muzzled dog can't catch the rat.

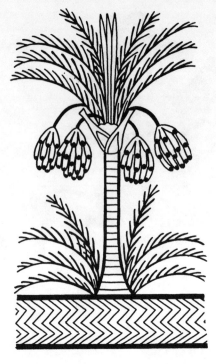

No matter how sharp a knife is, it cannot
carve its own hilt – YORUBA

There is no cunning person who ever licked
his own back – ZULU

We must hang up our bags where our hands
can reach – IGBO

You lift up an object as high as you are tall –
EWE

LISTENING

A good listener makes a single trip; a bad
listener makes fifty – HAITIAN

Advice is useful when one listens – IGBO

Ears are uninvited witnesses – TSWANA

Ears usually witness a matter without
invitation – TSWANA

First listen; be the last to speak – HAITIAN

Hasten to listen and be slow to speak – HAITIAN

One who has not listened to 'leave it alone' will listen to 'how do you feel?' – FULANI

If you are a good listener and you advise someone, she listens – TSHI

One must talk little, and listen much – WOLOF

The ear tells the heart – NDEBELE

The fault in every kind of character comes from not listening – ANCIENT EGYPTIAN

The one who listens is the one who understands – JABO

LONELINESS & SOLITARINESS

A bad person is better than an empty house – GA

Eat on your own is dying on your own – MAMPRUSSI

He who lives alone has no quarrel – KIKUYU

Loneliness is painful – TWI

The woods are not heartless (i.e. there is comfort in solitude) – SOUTHERN AFRICA

What you do on your own does not make you cry – SHONA

LOSS

A tree lopped of its branches does not move in the wind – EWE

She who lost something will be the one who will be looking for it – HAITIAN

If a thing is lost, we start looking for it at home – TSHI

The child whose mother died and the one whose mother went to market cry alike – GURAGE

There are breakages which cannot be replaced like a pot – KIKUYU

LOVE

[The] one who loves an unsightly person is the one who makes him beautiful – GANDA

A dead person is loved – SWAHILI

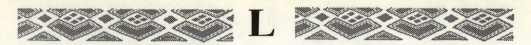

A loving heart doesn't fail to help – UGANDAN

A slap of love does not hurt – SWAHILI

Dem dat want fe lub mus' lub – JAMAICAN
They that want to love must love.

Fait' dare eberyting, and lub bear eberyting – JAMAICAN
Faith dares everything, and love bears everything.

He who is loved by his wife has no trouble conversing – MALAGASY

She who is loved receives no refusal – KIKUYU

He who loves you warns you – GANDA

He who loves, loves you with your dirt – UGANDAN

If you're really in love, you don't care if she's a virgin or not – HAITIAN

It is not enough to love if you are not loved in return – TSONGA

Love eats [i.e. destroys] the understanding – GANDA

Love enters even though it is forbidden – THONGA

Love has neither eyes nor understanding – SWAHILI

Love is a cover: it hides all shortcomings – SHONA

Love is love only when it affects both sides – SWAHILI

Love is the greatest of all virtues – TSHI

Love pardons all, self-pride nothing – HAITIAN

May your love not be like a stone: if it breaks you cannot put the pieces together. May your love be like iron: when it breaks you can weld the pieces back together – MALAGASY

One does not love another if one does not accept anything from him – KANURI

One who loves you does not spare you the truth – UGANDAN

One's lover's place is never too far away – KIKUYU

Our love opens the doors of our insight without our knowledge – SWAHILI

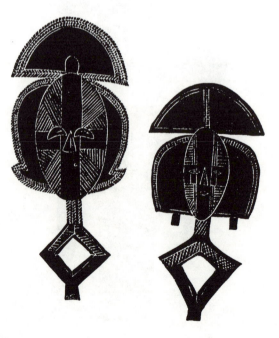

You know whom you love; you cannot know who loves you – **YORUBA**

You may condemn the one you love, but you pay his fine for him – **GANDA**

Di [the] blacker di berry, di sweeter di juice – **CREOLE (BELIZE)**

Di olda [older] di violin, di sweeta di music – **CREOLE (BELIZE)**

Real love knows not danger – **HAITIAN**

Tell me whom you love, and I'll tell you who you are – **LOUISIANA (CREOLE)**

The hyena does not eat its baby, and you know how insatiable it is – **KIKUYU**

The loved one has no faults – **SWAHILI**

The man who is not jealous in love, loves not – **TAMASHEK**

The one who gives you food is the one who loves you – **SWAHILI**

The way to the beloved is not thorny – **DUALA**

Their enquiring about your troubles doesn't mean that they love you – **MAMPRUSSI**

There is one who loves you after seeing you, and there is one who loves you unseen – **SWAHILI**

To love is not to be forced to love – **KIKUYU**

Truth should be in love and love in truth – **SWAHILI**

What you love, you make last long – **GANDA**

You do not know how to cry before your mother dies – **OVAMBO**

LUCK

A person's luck is his character or behaviour – SWAHILI

A wandering hunter encounters a wandering beast – EWE

Dog luck ent cat wun – BAJAN
The dog's luck isn't the cat's own.

Game will always appear on the side of the inexperienced hunters – TSWANA

Good and bad together are grist to the lucky man – HAUSA

If you shoot at an animal and it runs to your house, it helps you carry your meat – TSHI

It is a lucky accident when beans get burnt after they have been salted – SHONA

Luck goes where luck is – LUYIA

Luck is better than beauty – LUO

The accident-prone are struck by the very first arrow in their very first fight – UGANDAN

The day I go to hunt, the hare climbs up the trees – IGBO

The lucky eagle kills a mouse that has eaten salt – UGANDAN

The lucky person can sell water even on the river Niger – HAUSA

To be born with luck is much better than to be born of a good father – OROMO

When you're in ill-luck, a snake can bite you even with its tail – MARTINIQUE

When you're unlucky, a potato peel can cut your foot – HAITIAN

M

If you no got smile on you face, no use open shop – JAMAICAN

Giving badly is the same as absolutely refusing – LAMBA

If we go forward we die; if we go backward we die; better go forward and die – ZULU

Many presents given with bad grace, are not worth a few given with good grace – HAYA

The way she does it is good too – SUKUMA

To warn a man is not to scold him – GA

When you serve, serve well – SWAHILI

A dog that lets himself be tied deserves to be beaten – HAITIAN

Di stilles calf suck di mos' milk – CREOLE (BELIZE)
The stillest calf sucks the most milk.

Tree leaves go where the wind blows – MAMPRUSSI

MALICE

Spiteful man put peppah da he mout' fo' blow dutty out a-he matty yeye – GUYANAN
The spiteful man puts pepper in his mouth to blow dirt out of his friend's eye.

One who plans the downfall of another does not do so in his presence – YORUBA

MANNER

A genteel refusal is preferable to an uncivil gift – HAITIAN

All people will die, but we want a good death – TSHI

MANNERS

Etiquette is like a law – SWAHILI

Good manners is civilization – SWAHILI

If you visit the village of the toads and you find them squatting you must squat too – EWE

When you go to someone's house and she is squatting, you don't ask her for a chair – TSHI

When you go to where frogs stay you live as frogs do – SWAHILI

The child who is not afraid of anybody will develop bad manners – YORUBA

121

M

When one reaches a land where men cut off their ears, he cuts off his own – IGBO

MARRIAGE & COURTSHIP

A good live-wid bettah dan a bad marriage
– BAJAN
A good 'live with' is better than a bad marriage.

A woman married without consultation runs away without consultation – OROMO

Courtship is not marriage – UGANDAN

De same mout' dat court yuh don't marry yuh – BAJAN
The mouth that courts you doesn't marry you.

Getting married with a woman is nothing; it's assuming the responsibility of marriage that counts – HAITIAN

Husband is the tie, wife is the parcel: when the tie breaks, the parcel loosens – IGBO

If you marry a beautiful woman, you marry trouble – JABO

Marry fe [for] love, work fe money. [re appropriateness and motivation] – JAMAICAN

One who is looking for a wife doesn't speak contemptuously of women – TSHI

The man who says he will not marry a woman with other admirers, will not marry a woman – YORUBA

The way you got married is not the way you'll get divorced – HAITIAN

MATURITY & IMMATURITY

Forbearance is maturity – SWAHILI

If we have not the qualities of age we appear to be youths – YORUBA

It is not [by] height [that] I know the maturity of my child – IGBO

Maturity or old age sweetens a banana fruit but not the human being – HAYA

When a child speaks, his maturity is portrayed – IGBO

When a girl outgrows 'who is the father?' the question will be 'who is the husband?.' – IGBO

You have grown up in body only, your heart within is that of a little child – LAMBA

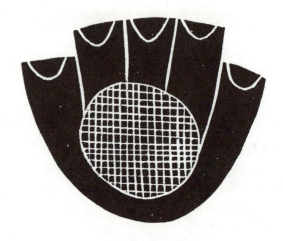

THE MEAN & THE MISERLY

Death has the key to the miser's chest – **TSHI**

Don' leh one drop o' tar mek yuh lose yuh whole ship an' cargo – **BAJAN**
Don't let one drop of tar make you lose your whole ship and cargo.

How is it that the rich only are niggardly? – **MALAGASY**

The dog's god is the bit of food that falls to the ground – **BONDEI**

The miser's goods are eaten by mice – **TSHI**

Death has the key to open the miser's chest – **ASHANTI**

Make a request and discover the unwilling; go a-begging and discover the miser – **YORUBA**

MEANS

A cutlass that is very sharp cannot of its own cut grass; a man has to handle it – **YORUBA**

A knife without a handle cannot carve – **SWAHILI**

A small key opens a big padlock – **SWAHILI**

A thorn has pierced you in the wilds: and then you take another thorn to get out the one which has pierced you – **GANDA**

De same 'tick wha lick black snake wi' lick yalla one – **JAMAICAN**
The same stick that beats the black snake will beat the yellow one.

De same hammah wah dribe nail sa tek am out – **GUYANAN**
The same hammer that drives the nail in will it out.

Follow the bee so that you may eat honey – **SWAHILI**

For a crooked hole a crooked probe – **FULANI**

He who has an axe does not lack firewood – **SWAHILI**

If you drink soup you lub [love] [s]'poon – **JAMAICAN**

It is a small thing that is taken to measure a big thing – **TSHI**

It is the ear that penetrates through darkness, not the eye – **MAASAI**

The Hima cow spears the way her horns are shaped – **UGANDAN**

The knife for flaying an elephant does not need to be a big one as long as it is sharp – HAUSA

The man that has the sharp knife is the one that will eat the meat – SWAHILI

The path you climb up is the same one you must come down – TSHI

When man hab [has] raw meat him look fe [for] fire – JAMAICAN

With shoes one can get on in the midst of thorns – YORUBA

Without teeth no bone can be broken – SWAHILI

You cannot cross the ocean by swimming – SWAHILI

You cannot hold a rod and still allow a dog to bite you – YORUBA

If you want to catch a monkey, you have to behave like one – YORUBA

MEMORY & REMEMBRANCE

A parent dies in the body, but not in the minds of the children – GANDA

An action is forgotten by the doer, but the receiver never forgets it – SWAHILI

By remembering the past, the future is remembered – OROMO

Do not observe what is before and forget what is behind – SWAHILI

It is always easier to remember refusals than gifts – KIKUYU

Memory reaches further than the eyes – KANURI

What we are remembered by is the work we have done – IGBO

Where a hawk has eaten a chick it does not forget – SHONA

Yesterday does not pass away – THONGA

A hyena does not forget where it ate a bone – TONGA

A man cannot undo his past. Can zebras wipe away their stripes? – NAMIBIAN

Last year's coldness has gone together with its firewood – HAUSA

Seeing the ashes you will never imagine how bright the fire was – HAYA

M

The past is far away – **TSONGA**

Whoever recalls last year has not found anything good in this year – **HAUSA**

Yesterday is buried – **NDEBELE**

The teeth may smile but the heart doesn't forget – **UGANDAN**

MEN

Boasting and a male cannot be separated – **MAASAI**

It is because of man [that] we wear swords – **TSHI**

Na [not] all man a-wear trouses [trousers] a man – **GUYANAN**

No man is a hero to his woman – **SWAHILI**

The rabbit has a saying which goes: 'If you were born a male, then you are given impossible tasks.' – **TSHI**

The tears of a man drop on to his chest. (A man will cry with head lowered so that others may not see his tears) – **NDEBELE**

What is pleasant to an animal may be bitter to a man – **NANDI**

MEN & WOMEN

Man build house, but woman mek [makes] de [the] home – **JAMAICAN**

Men and women towards each other are for the eyes and for the heart, and not only for the bed – **TAMASHEK**

He who is ashamed to sleep with his wife will not have children – **ANCIENT EGYPTIAN**

MERIT

He who does not give should not take – **YORUBA**

She who does well will be paid likewise – **SWAHILI**

One who sings only one song will get only one penny – **HAITIAN**

If man milk cow, he mus'[t] drink milk – **GUYANAN**

Into the mouth of a useless dog often falls a tasty bone – **SHONA**

It is what you plant that you reap – **YORUBA**

Laugh at a deformed person and you will bear a deformed child – **SWAHILI**

No ketchee [catch], no habee [have] – **GUYANAN**

The chakata fruit on the ground belongs to all, but the one on the tree is for she who can climb – **SHONA**

The digger of the well is not forbidden the water – **SWAHILI**

The head that provokes the wasp, that head will get the sting – **IGBO**

The hoe does not steal where it has been cultivating – **GANDA**

The person whose head is used to break the coconut will not wait to eat from it – **YORUBA**

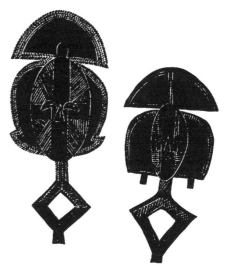

The way a person eats is the way she or he works – OVAMBO

What you deserve, you don't have to ask for – HAITIAN

What you sow, that you reap – OVAMBO

You spread you bed hard, you mus' hab fe lie hard 'pon i' – JAMAICAN
You spread your bed hard, you must lie hard upon it.

MISFORTUNE

A man on the ground cannot fall – THONGA

A misfortune borne patiently is as though it had not been – HAUSA

A water-pot breaks just outside the door – LUYIA

Affliction does not leave a place which is already known – KIKUYU

An accident does not ask for permission to enter – SWAHILI

An accident does not knock at the door – SWAHILI

Betta fe fall from window dan roof – JAMAICAN
Better to fall from the window than from the roof.

Don't laugh at a blind man: it is not his fault – SWAHILI

Even on a good path you can stub your toe – SUKUMA

Good days are soon forgotten, bad ones never – IDOMA

He flees from the roaring lion to the crouching lion – TSWANA

If the little stump in the path does not trip you when you are going, it trips you when you are going back – GANDA

It's the child who draws water who breaks the pot – MAMPRUSSI

Mischief come by de [the] pound an'[d] go by de ounce – JAMAICAN

Running from the smoke into the fire – TEMNE

Someone escaped being [hit] by the spear but has fallen by the arrow – SWAHILI

The drum that beats well is the one that breaks – KAONDE

The hen of a poor man does not lay, and if she lays she does not hatch – SWAHILI

M

The tree that you have cut has fallen on the water that you drink – **KAONDE**

While running from the rain, you fall into a stream – **HAITIAN**

You will meet the cobra when you have no stick – **NAMIBIAN**

MISTAKES

Better a mistake at the beginning than at the end – **FULANI**

Erring is of a courageous person – **KIKUYU**

Even a clever person makes mistakes: the ears do not catch a sweet smell – **UGANDAN**

If a child goes [on] an errand wrongly, she will go again – **IGBO**

One error brings on another – **HAITIAN**

The curse at the barren cow hit the pregnant one instead – **UGANDAN**

To err is human – **SHONA**

To lose your way is one way of finding it – **SWAHILI**

To miss the trail is to know the trail – **SUKUMA**

You in de [the] right church but in de wrong pew – **JAMAICAN**

MODERATION

Don't climb too high, don't go too far down; take the middle course – **HAITIAN**

If your cloth is dirty, you wash it, you don't burn it – **TSHI**

One doesn't beat a dog until his teeth fall out – **JABO**

To be hard does not mean to be hard as a stone, and to be soft does not mean to be soft as water – **KIKUYU**

To pull the hand out of the hole in the tree is to soften the hand – **KAONDE**

When belly full, jaw mus'[t] [s]'top – **JAMAICAN**

A frown is not a slap – **HAUSA**

A stumble is not a fall – HAITIAN

Do not mourn a woman whose newly-born baby has died, and forget one who has died together with her baby – SHONA

It is only the water that is spilt; the calabash is not broken – YORUBA

Wha' good fuh de sick bettah fuh de well – BAJAN
What's good for the sick is better for the well.

'You are ugly' is different from 'you are very ugly.' – TSHI

MONEY & THRIFT

Be ready wid [with] you[r] hat, but slow wid you money – JAMAICAN

Buying a horse for fifty, and not being able to buy a saddle for five – OROMO

Cheap t'[h]ing mek [makes] all man buy – GUYANAN

Dere's [there's] no lock golden key no [can't] open – JAMAICAN

Hab [have] money, hab fren' [friend] – JAMAICAN

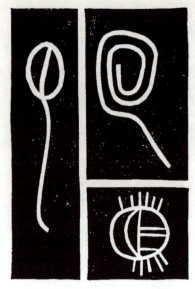

She who is patient with a 'farthing' will see a thousand – HAUSA

If one wants to eat, she asks her purse – TSHI

If a place is dark and then money is scattered there, it becomes light – TSHI

If someone says he will give you something sweet to eat and he gives you money, he has done it – TSHI

It takes money to make money – HAITIAN

Love of money is the root of all evil – TSHI

Money can crack stones – HAITIAN

Money earns more money – TSONGA

Money is a sharp knife – IGBO

Money is blood.[i.e. it brings trouble] – HAITIAN

Money is like a fool: it accepts [being] possessed by anybody – SHONA

Money is like a slave, if you don't treat it well, it flees – TSHI

Money is not counted well for you by somebody else – GANDA

M

Money is respect – HAITIAN

Money knows no day on which it is not welcome – SHONA

Money na [doesn't] a-grow [u]'pon tree – GUYANAN

Money na [doesn't] mek [make] man – GUYANAN

Money shortens any topic or controversy – IGBO

Pu'[r]se full, plenty frien'[d] – GUYANAN

Sabe [save] money and money sabe you – JAMAICAN

Savings will not rot – SWAHILI

The size of your purse is the measure of your charm – HAITIAN

When there is no money, there are no ornaments – MALAGASY

When two people have a common purse, one sings and the other weeps – SWAHILI

When you're penniless, you understand the value of money – HAITIAN

With money we wash off bad luck – IGBO

Food can be refused after I have had my fill but not money – SHONA

Manage good better dan [than] big wage – JAMAICAN

To dispense with what is not customary is not economy – FULANI

MOTHERS

A mother is not to be compared with another person - she is incomparable – MONGO

A wife is for a certain time, your mother is for always – HAITIAN

Better my mother's lumpy gruel than my step-mother's smooth porridge – UGANDAN

Even if you hate your mother, you do not hand her over to the enemy – TSHI

He who takes anything to his mother, never says that it is too heavy – GANDA

If a child takes [an] interest in crying, its mother will develop [an] interest in comforting it – YORUBA

If the mother is good, the child will be good – HAITIAN

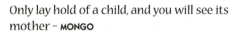

beer each day cause not her to raise her hands to God in complaint of thee – ANCIENT EGYPTIAN

MOTIVES & MOTIVATION

That which lives in the hole has reason to live there – IGBO

The love that is shown to the cock is necessitated by the wish to include its meat among the ingredients for a stew – YORUBA

The one who warms herself at the fire while the sun is shining, does so for some reason – KIKUYU

The stranger who wants to befriend you has noticed your pretty sister – UGANDAN

The vulture does not circle without reason – KAMBA

There are people who [help] place a basket on your head to see what you carry – WOLOF

Hog run fe [for] him life, darg [dog] run fe him character – JAMAICAN

A person does not object to being called, she objects to what she is called for – SWAHILI

Only lay hold of a child, and you will see its mother – MONGO

The mother is she who catches the knife by the blade.[i.e. in protecting the child from attack] – TSWANA

Though your mother be poor, she is still your mother – OVAMBO

Thy mother carried thee for months, she suckled thee for three years, when thou wast at school she brought thee bread and

N

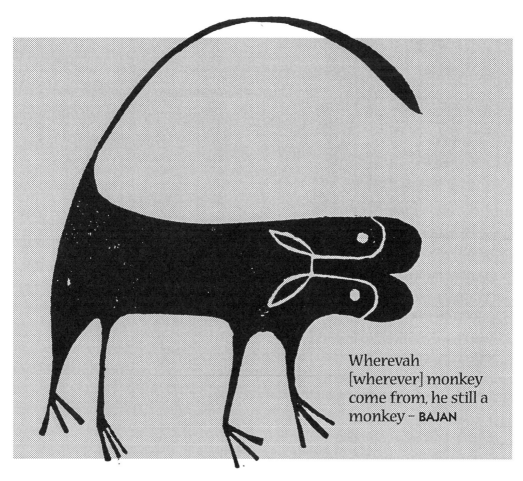

Wherevah [wherever] monkey come from, he still a monkey – **BAJAN**

NAMES

A child's name influences its behaviour – **YORUBA**

A name or a nickname influences one's character – **YORUBA**

In order to find out evil-doers, every human being is given a name – **TWI**

The owner of a name knows his name, you say to the thief 'stop thief!' and he bolts – **HAUSA**

If you inherit a name you must also adopt its affairs – **SWAHILI**

NATURE

A doctor cannot cure [a] natural defect – **IGBO**

A dog's curled tail cannot be made straight – **TSONGA**

A flag follows the wind – **SWAHILI**

A hawk, even if a cow is killed for him, its eye is still where a chicken is – **IGBO**

A lion is a lion even if it eats grass – **SWAHILI**

A thorn tree will bear thorns – **KIKUYU**

Cutting the ears of a mule will not make him a horse – **LOUISIANA (CREOLE)**

Even if the tooth of the snake is dead, if you step on its tooth, the tooth bites – **KAONDE**

Even where there is no cock, it dawns – **NDEBELE**

For every rose flower, there is a thorn – **IGBO**

Hawk's brood will always be hawkish – **SWAHILI**

If a log lies on the bottom of the river for a thousand years it never changes into a crocodile – **TSHI**

If rain beats a leopard he becomes wet, but the spots of his body are not washed off – **TSHI**

If you change the rat into a squirrel, it doesn't change – **TSHI**

Light is the enemy of darkness – **SWAHILI**

Man weapon a-he [is his] fist, woman weapon a-he [is her] tongue – **GUYANAN**

Mice can only breed mice – **TSWANA**

Na de lacking ob a tongue mek cow can't talk – **GUYANAN**
It's not the lacking of a tongue that makes the cow unable to talk.

No matter how thoroughly a crow may wash, it remains ever black – **SHONA**

No one teaches a leopard's cub how to spring – **ASHANTI**

Puss may look 'pon king, but him rader ratta – **JAMAICAN**
A cat may look upon a king, but he would rather look upon a rat.

That which will bear fruits gives out flowers first – **SWAHILI**

The child of a snake is a snake – **SWAHILI**

The crocodile's child does not die by drowning – **EWE**

The cub of a lion is a lion – **NDEBELE**

The gazelle jumps, and should her child crawl? – **FULFULDE**

The night is over before one has finished counting the stars! – **FIPA**

There is nothing we can do for the pig to stop it wallowing in the mire – **YORUBA**

The tiger may get old, but his claws get sharper – **HAITIAN**

Though a mouse were as big as a bullock, yet it would be the slave of the cat – **OJI**

Though hornless, still a cow – **OVAMBO**

Where good things go, from there good things return – **SWAHILI**

Where the sea is there the rivers lead – **SWAHILI**

You gib darg little in a plate, him tek it out put 'pon grung – **JAMAICAN**
You give the dog a little in a plate, he takes it out and puts it upon the ground.

You may be clever, but you can never lose your shadow – **IGBO**

If the stream is not checked it will cross the road – **TSHI**

A rose is surrounded by thorns – **SWAHILI**

The wind that is contrary when you're going is fine when you return – **HAITIAN**

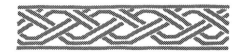 

In the evening even a copper-coloured person looks black – TSHI

A person is trapped by what she likes most – IGBO

If the elephant were not in the wilderness, buffalo would be the greatest – JABO

NECESSITY

A panting animal will stop under any tree – KIKUYU

A spring is not a chief, yet whoever would drink of it must bow – SWAHILI

Do it though you do not want to – OVAMBO

Does anybody refuse to sleep to avoid nightmares? – UGANDAN

Even a rich man is in need of a needle – EWE

One who goes into the sea must swim – SWAHILI

She who has necessity has no shame – KIKUYU

He who wants what is under the bed must stoop for it – SWAHILI

How cunning is the hare when chased by dogs – TSONGA

If all [its] needs were solely on the ground, the monkey wouldn't have made the tree-top its house – IGBO

If everybody is told not to move, the person whose position is not all right must move – IGBO

If the lion is hungry it will eat grass – NDEBELE

If you don't sleep you can't dream – TSHI

If you nyam egg you mus' bruk de shell – JAMAICAN
If you eat an egg you must break the shell.

Necessity makes the donkey run faster than a horse – HAITIAN

No matter how beautiful the shoes are, they still have to go on the ground – HAITIAN

No rain no rainbow – JAMAICAN

One who has lost something never searches only one place – SWAHILI

Poverty breeds knowledge – AFRICAN

The foot and the earth cannot help meeting – KIKUYU

The fruit must have a stem before it grows – JABO

The lion made me climb a tree of thorns – AFRICAN

The needy is the one who takes initiatives – HAYA

To warm oneself is to feed the fire – KIKUYU

When you are hungry eat what you despise, and when you are sated, despise it – ANCIENT EGYPTIAN

When you meet a snake, make sure you kill it outright – NAMIBIAN

Where the cow is tied is where she's going to shit – HAITIAN

You cannot do without water even if it drowned your child – OVAMBO

You have to plough with the oxen that you have – **HAITIAN**

You kill the snake with whatever may be in your hand – **JABO**

You know how to drink water before you drink palm wine – **TSHI**

NEED

The person draws near to the fire whose meat is raw – **KANURI / BORNU**

She who asks has a need to know – **SWAHILI**

He who has need is not shy – **KIKUYU**

One who needs a thing will travel on a bad road to get it – **TSHI**

It is the person who has the thorn in her foot who limps to the person who will help her extract it – **YORUBA**

Need breaks need – **SWAHILI**

Sick man look fo'[r] dactah [doctor] – **GUYANAN**

What is wanted is what is done – **MAMPRUSSI**

When man belly full him bruk [break] pot – **JAMAICAN**

NEIGHBOURS

A neighbour nearby is better than a relative far away – **SWAHILI**

Don' discommode yuhself tuh sideboard yuh neighbour – **BAJAN**

Don't inconvenience yourself to accommodate your neighbour.

What is bad for you is not good for your neighbour – **SWAHILI**

What you do not like, do not do unto your neighbour – **TWI**

When the fire goes out you re-light [it] from your neighbour's: do the same with wisdom – **UGANDAN**

NEWS

If the ear does not hear the news, the mind does not become unhappy – **IGBO**

News don'[t] lack a carrier – **BAJAN**

The tortoise said if the old things happen, do not call her; but if a new thing happens, call her – **IGBO**

Where you do not walk, your ears walk – **HAYA**

O

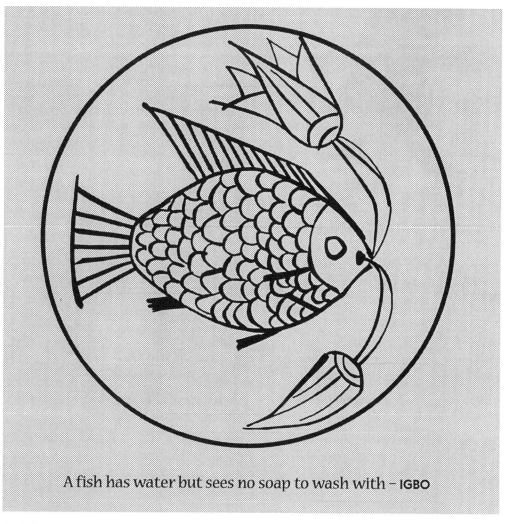

A fish has water but sees no soap to wash with – IGBO

OBSERVATION

De more yuh [you] watch, de less yuh see – BAJAN

She who walks in front of you gives you wisdom – GANDA

If you bend forward to look at somebody from beneath, someone else is also looking at you from beneath – EWE

To look too hard is to become blind – FIPA

One seeks things where they are to be found – HAYA

The eye is not a measure but it knows short weight – HAUSA

OLD AGE

An old person has eaten wisdom – OVAMBO

'Don't you know I was like you?' said the old, dry leaf to the proud young one – UGANDAN

Grow old, body, the heart still remains –
NDEBELE

The one who used to jump across the
stream may find herself wading through –
KIKUYU

You can run away from your elder, but she'll
outthink you – **SUKUMA**

She who thinks that old people are not wise
has insulted many people – **YORUBA**

If you wish good advice, consult the old
persons – **OROMO**

The child looks everywhere and often sees
nought; but the old man, sitting on the
ground, sees everything – **WOLOF**

OPPORTUNITY

A person who is always looking in the sky
will never discover anything on the ground
– **EWE**

A tree drops nothing on those who are not
there – **SWAHILI**

Fields without owners are reaped by
passers-by – **UGANDAN**

Fruit falls where there are no gatherers –
FIPA

Game appears to the one without a bow –
LAMBA

Good things don't come to market only once
– **IGBO**

One who waits for chance may wait a year –
YORUBA

If God carves a drum for you, then the act of
beating it is your job – **IGBO**

If I pour water on you, then wash yourself –
TEMNE

If none seek them, opportunities will not be
found – **FULANI**

If the hare has outwitted the hunters today,
tomorrow is still a hunting day – **IGBO**

Rain nebber fall a' one man door – **JAMAICAN**
Rain never falls at one man's door.

Soup col', daag put mout' deh – **GUYANAN**
When the soup is cold the dog puts his mouth there.

The mouth that does not eat is an invitation
to the mouth that does eat – **SOTHO**

The sun does not rise for one person alone –
OVAMBO

The sun does not wait for the traveller –
KIKUYU

There are many dawns – **TSWANA**

Today it's me, tomorrow it's you – **GIRIAMA**

Today's rich person is not the last – **YORUBA**

Watchman a de biges' tief – **JAMAICAN**
The watchman is the biggest thief.

What is built on chance is built on sand –
HAITIAN

When a bowl of food drops it is luck for the
dog – **GIRIAMA**

When it (the sun) comes out, bask in it –
SWAHILI

When meat is put on the dish take your share – **UGANDAN**

When the spoon takes a holiday, the spider makes his web in the stew-pot – **YORUBA**

Where the child with a mother is being advised [by her mother], there does the motherless child learn her own lessons – **IGBO**

Your world is while you are in it – **HAUSA**

OPPRESSION

Chicken-hawk say, he can't get mamma, he tek [take] picknie [the chick] – **GUYANAN**

When the goat was told that the head butcher was dead she said 'Oh! has the butcher's knife died with him?' – **HAUSA**

Who oppresses the weak is a reproach to his maker – **IGBO**

ORIGINS

A complete article must have gone through various stages in its creation – **HAYA**

A transplanted tree doesn't resemble a sown tree – **MAMPRUSSI**

A tree is strong because of the roots – **KAONDE**

Coconut tree, no matter how tall it grows, it is from the ground – **IGBO**

However old a tree may be, the soil is older – **IGBO**

The 'amanne' tree grows down in the ground before it grows tall – **TSHI**

When a tree dies at its roots, its branches dry up also – **SWAHILI**

However far the stream flows, it never forgets its source – **YORUBA**

OTHERS

A matter that concerns other people should not be kept to oneself – **YORUBA**

A person trying to kill a snake should remember that the snake also wants to live – **IGBO**

A pole is strengthened by another pole – **THONGA**

An arrow-head in someone else's body is nothing but an arrow-shaft – **JUKUN**

But for the knee, the leg could not bend – **MONGO**

Everyone thinks that the other one's burden is a dry leaf – **SWAHILI**

One who does not know the road delays one that knows it – **KIKUYU**

The person whose greetings do not make one feel happy cannot make one unhappy by not greeting – **YORUBA**

If it is awarded to her, she has been favoured; if it is awarded to me, I deserve it – **SWAHILI**

O

If the sickness is in your friend, it's outside your body – SUKUMA

If you lub [love] good fe [for] yourself, you must lub i'[t] fe you fren' [friend] – JAMAICAN

If you want to understand anybody, go with him on a journey – LUYIA

It is not necessary to blow out the other person's lantern to let yours shine – SWAHILI

It is the influence of the fountain that causes the stream to flow – YORUBA

Many small rivers make the ocean big – TSHI

One head cannot hold a consultation – TSHI

One who sends someone to fight will not give him strength – IGBO

Remember that you didn't get there by yourself – HAITIAN

Rings sound when there are two – NDEBELE

[The] madness of another person's brother is funny – IGBO

The road that is good, is not good for one person only – IGBO

The tree is full of fruit, but do not think that it is fertile by itself: they have ploughed around it – TSONGA

The way it's with you, it's like that with everyone – MAMPRUSSI

Through others I am somebody – TSWANA

We are people because of other people – SOTHO

What you don't like, don't do to your neighbour – TSHI

When it is not your mother who is in danger of being eaten by the wild animal, the matter can wait until the morrow – GANDA

When you put you[r] han'[d] in you own floor [flour] barrel you put it a[t] you wrist, when you put it in you neighbour['s] you put it a you elbow – JAMAICAN

Wisdom, cunning, skill or knowledge is not for one person only – ACHOLI

Without a third person to intervene, two [people] may fight to [the] death – YORUBA

You can't snap your fingers without your thumb – IGBO

You need a mirror to see a blot on the face – SWAHILI

P

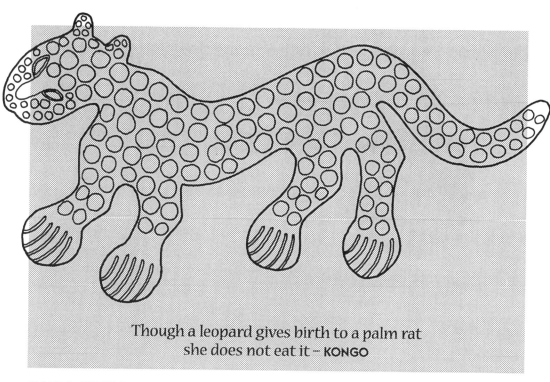

Though a leopard gives birth to a palm rat
she does not eat it – KONGO

PARASITES

'Can I manage a small space?' is the first move
of a parasite before becoming an occupier of
the house – YORUBA

Lizard no plant corn but him hab [have]
plenty – BAHAMIAN

When money done [finished], lub [love] done
– JAMAICAN

PARENTS & PARENTHOOD

A bad habit picked up by a child may be
corrected, [but] not one coming from its
parents – UGANDAN

A donkey can't breed a horse – MAMPRUSSI

A hen with chicks does not know how to run
away in time of danger – NIGERIAN

A parent is merciful – KIKUYU

Although a baboon is fearful, it does not
allow its young one to be touched – SHONA

He who has neither father nor mother has no
wisdom – OVAMBO

One who has borne children ought to be
patient – SHONA

One who loves the children of his fellow will
surely love his own children – JABO

Parents are merciful – KIKUYU

Parents give birth to the body of their
children, but not always to their characters –
GANDA

The bitch never bites her pups to the bone –
HAITI

P

A patient person gains at last – **IGBO**

A patient woman has all the wealth that there is in this world – **JABO**

One who walks slowly gets far – **LUYIA**

A tree that has grown bent for thirty years cannot be straightened in one year – **TSHI**

An elephant does not grow in one day – **GIO**

At the bottom of patience there is heaven – **KANURI / BORNU**

Do not be impatient when you question, so that you get angry when it is time to listen – **ANCIENT EGYPTIAN**

Eat a grasshopper's head while waiting for a bull's steak – **KALENJIN**

Height is not to be hurried – **NDEBELE**

If patience hides something, anger won't search and get – **MAMPRUSSI**

'If you delay, you will get what is in the world – **MAMPRUSSI**

If you find the river flooded, wait – **SWAHILI**

If you patiently endure, you come out victorious – **TWI**

The chicken with children doesn't swallow the worm – **SUKUMA**

The foot of the hen does not kill its chick – **TSHI**

The hen is dead, the eggs rot – **TSONGA**

The parent has no ill temper – **KIKUYU**

They beget the body, they do not beget the heart – **TSONGA**

Wha'[t] de [the] goat do, de kid follow – **JAMAICAN**

You do not know that you love your parents until they die – **NAMIBIAN**

He that fears lest his child cry, will cry himself – **SWAHILI**

The soft-hearted [parent] hardens the child – **UGANDAN**

The vine follows the pole. [parents and children] – **HAITIAN**

PATIENCE & TOLERANCE
'Soon' doesn't mean tomorrow – **HAITIAN**

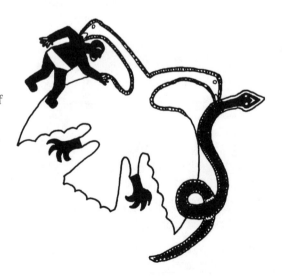

P

One straw becomes a bird's nest – **OVAMBO**

Patience is corn in the pot: it finishes very quickly – **HAUSA**

The water which is ahead does not help quench the thirst – **KIKUYU**

Patience is the best of dispositions: one who possesses patience, possesses all things – **YORUBA**

Patience without resentment results in good steering – **ANCIENT EGYPTIAN**

Small drops will fill a river – **KORANKO**

The news of the evening may triumph over that of the morning – **MAASAI**

There is no need to rattle a parcel that will soon be opened – **IGBO**

What is hot will eventually get cold – **IGBO**

What you lose in the fire, you will find in the ashes – **MARTINIQUE**

Where the rabbit goes, there also will the tortoise reach – **MAMPRUSSI**

With patience one achieves more than with anger – **HO**

With patience you can see a louse's belly-button – **HAITIAN**

Bear with a fool, there is foolishness in you too – **OVAMBO**

If you put up with a leopard, put up with its scratches – **UGANDAN**

Too much tolerance paves the way for trouble – **KIKUYU**

They who live together must be merciful – **KIKUYU**

PEACE

A peace-maker often receives wounds – **YORUBA**

If a person loves peace, it does not make her or him a coward – **IGBO**

If two people fight, the third one is the peacemaker – **TSHI**

In tranquillity lies danger – **LOZI**

It is better to build bridges than walls – **SWAHILI**

If you wish to keep peace, sometimes you have to make concessions – **HAITIAN**

One does not like heat and the other does not like cold; make it tepid and still be friends – MALAGASY

PERSEVERANCE

A man who lets his problems get the better of him is like a man who divorces his wife the first time she makes him angry – MALAGASY

If cases don't stop coming you don't stop sitting in judgement – TSHI

If he who is running after you is not tired, then you who are running away don't say: 'I am tired.' – TSHI

If you are clean don't stop washing – HAUSA

Little by little the mouse finishes the hide – SUKUMA

Nothing is impossible to a woman of will – KIKUYU

Perseverance wins the battle – LUO

The persistent drop rots the spot [upon which] it falls – UGANDAN

The quick one may not win, the enduring one will – TSWANA

To fall and rise up again is the journey of this world – IGBO

Where there is bending there will be rising up – SWAHILI

PERSPECTIVE

A matter which in one place causes laughter, at another place causes tears – TSHI

An unpleasant matter should be seen from an unpleasant viewpoint – YORUBA

She who knows us is not like her we know – YORUBA

Hog run for him life; dog run for him character – BAHAMIAN

It is playing for children and [an] emergency for the butterfly – OROMO

The death of one man means a good drink for another – HAITIAN

The executioner and the person destined to be killed do not sleep – TSHI

The pastimes of the cats mean tears for the mice – HAITIAN

The slave weeps because she is sold for money but her owner weeps because he got too little money (her price) – OROMO

The small gazelle runs to save its life, but the dog chases to fill its belly – OROMO

What hurts some, helps others – HAITIAN

What is fun to the small boy is death to a frog – AFRICAN

Your joy is my grief – SWAHILI

Your play is our death – SWAHILI

When an old thing belonging to one person gets into another person's hands it is a new thing to her – TSHI

P

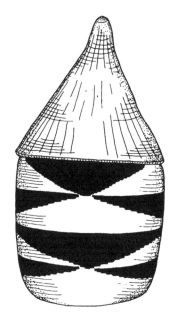

When a person's misery doesn't stop, you don't stop pitying her – TSHI

When killing a handsome person do not look at his face – GIRIAMA

PLAY

If you don't play, you can't win – HAITIAN

One should not, for a jest, take the arrow out of the quiver – KIKUYU

Play wid tigah picknie, but na play wid 'e mamma – GUYANAN
Play with the tiger cub, but don't play with the tigress.

There are toys for every age – HAITIAN

POSSESSION & PROPERTY

A bird flies off with only what it has swallowed – KIKUYU

A bird in the hand is better than a goose on the wing – HAITIAN

Wild bird owns the tree top and antelope owns the road – IGBO

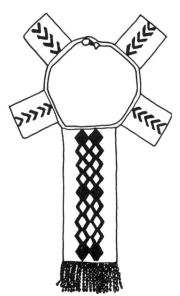

PERVERSENESS

A tale-bearer speaks quietly as if the surrounding bush would publicise her tales, whereas it is the person to whom she is whispering [that] will give them publicity – YORUBA

As the sick man was told to go slowly, was he told not to reach his house? – IGBO

'If we use the turkey as a bait, which bird do we wish to catch? – YORUBA

Kick darg [dog] him fren [befriend] you, feed him him bite you – JAMAICAN

When you gave him he refused, but when you placed it back he stole and finished it – OROMO

There is she who fears blame, yet she commits a great crime – ANCIENT EGYPTIAN

PITY

A person who knows you pities you – HAYA

one who has not suffered does not know how to pity – GANDA

P

An egg in the mouth is better than chickens in the nest – **NIGERIAN**

An egg today is better than a chicken tomorrow – **HAITIAN**

Bad meat is better than no meat – **GANDA**

Every one acquires property; it is a wise person who knows how to protect it – **ANCIENT EGYPTIAN**

Gold in one's hand looks like copper – **GURAGE**

Goods injure their owners by making them vain – **TSWANA**

She despises what he owns – **OVAMBO**

She who lives on her own land, lives as she pleases – **GANDA**

It is not acquisition that is difficult, it is retention – **MAASAI**

Man hab [have] cow him look fe [for] milk – **JAMAICAN**

One cowry of thine own is better than thy father's or mother's million – **HAUSA**

Quick cent bettah mo''an slow dallah – **GUYANAN**
A quick cent is better than a slow dollar.

To harvest is not so difficult as to keep the harvest – **KIKUYU**

What is your own is your own even if it is bad – **SWAHILI**

You might possess little, but what you possess is yours – **GANDA**

Your little is greater than someone's much – **MAMPRUSSI**

Your own little place is better than your neighbour's big place – **SWAHILI**

Your own rags excel another's garment – **HAUSA**

What a man possesses is not stronger than himself – **KANURI**

When gold is close to you, it is pale (no longer glitters) – **ASHANTI**

As soon as you obtain it (something precious) it loses its beauty – **TSHI**

Don't entrust your friend with what is not yours – **UGANDAN**

It is easier to prevent somebody from entering your home than from leaving it – **GANDA**

One whom you won't make pay a fine: don't let him spoil your property – **GANDA**

POTENTIAL & THE POSSIBLE

A little path can lead far away – HAITIAN

A shrub may grow into a tree – JUKUN

A small despised pot will boil over and put out the fire – IGBO

A spark burns down the forest – OVAMBO

All women's breasts can feed wise children – TSWANA

As you don't know which dog will hunt, train them all – UGANDAN

Despised in her own village, she may yet become famous in the world – NAMIBIAN

No one knows the direction and shape of a calf's future horns – UGANDAN

What is tried may become true – OVAMBO

Where a small thing comes from, there a big thing comes from – JABO

POVERTY

The indigestion of the rich avenges the hunger of the poor – HAITIAN

'What shall I add for the poor?' asked God. 'Fingernails and itch,' answered the poor – OROMO

A hen is the poor man's cow – NIGERIAN

A house of nothing but mud: the conflagration turns away in shame – HAUSA

A poor person has no friends – GANDA

A poor man's goat does not produce and if it does, it produces a barren goat – SWAHILI

If a poor person has nothing else, at least she has a tongue with which to defer the payment of her debts – TSHI

If a poor man insists on giving advice to a rich man, he would be termed mad – KURIA

If a poor person makes a proverb it does not spread – TSHI

If someone curses you saying: 'Let her die,' it is not as painful as saying, 'Let her become poor.' – TSHI

If you don't want to resign yourself to poverty, resign yourself to work – HAUSA

It is better to be poor in youth than in old age – KURIA

It is not only poverty that is disgraceful – TSHI

Man po'[or], him wud [word] po.' – JAMAICAN

Poor people can't afford to get sick – HAITIAN

Poor people entertain with the heart – HAITIAN

Poverty is like a lion, if you do not fight you get eaten – HAYA

P

The hen of a poor person does not lay eggs, and even if she lays eggs, she never hatches, and if she hatches, she never rears the chicks, and when she rears, the chicks are taken by the hawk – SWAHILI

The monkey says that there is nothing like poverty for taking the conceit out of a man – ASHANTI

The one who is poor but owes nothing is not poor – KIKUYU

The only cow of a poor person is the one that falls into a hole – UGANDAN

The poor man gets a friend; the rich man takes him away – IGBO

The poor man's word is considered last – ZULU

Wealth is invited but poverty invites itself – SHONA

When a poor man cries for help, only God will aid him – OVAMBO

When a poor man is decked out in gold, people say it is brass – ASHANTI

When the discussion refers to money, the poor man closes his mouth – IGBO

When you are suffering from poverty and happen to [fall] into cold water, it scalds you – TSHI

You become wise when you begin to run out of money – TSHI

Beggar beg from beggar him nebbar [never] get rich – JAMAICAN

Begging from a beggar is the height of misery – UGANDAN

Food that is begged never satisfies – SWAHILI

POWER

A chief's oath is like the hole a yam is planted in, no one falls into it and gets out again unhurt – TSHI

146

P

A path with thorns is the one leading to chieftanship – SHONA

A strong man beats you with the stick which you had in your own hands – GANDA

Do not mix your cattle with those of a chief – SHONA

Every power is subject to another power – SHONA

God is usually on the side of the chiefs – TSWANA

She who feeds you keeps an eye on you – LUYIA

He will fry you with your own oil – TEMNE

If an elephant steps on a trap that is set, it doesn't spring back – TSHI

If you follow the elephant, you never get entangled in the forest – TWI

No one who is following an elephant has to knock the dew of the grass – ASHANTI

One can wield a knife only where an elephant is already dead. Who dares do so in the presence of a living elephant? – YORUBA

One who has strength, she has the truth – MAMPRUSSI

One who surpasses another takes what he has; it is as if he gives him things to hold – IGBO

Small rudda [rudder] control big ship – CREOLE (BELIZE)

The axe of a strong man is fetched by a strong man – ACHOLI

The big ones eat the small ones – SWAHILI

The creeper which is as thick as a palm tree cannot stop an elephant; the creeper which tells an elephant not to pass must accompany the elephant on its way – YORUBA

The elephant destroys those who are near it – ZULU

The elephant does not take flight at the sight of a dog. Even the owner of two hundred dogs cannot chase an elephant – YORUBA

The elephant is not overpowered by its tusks – KIKUYU

The favourite food of your master is your favourite food – TWI

The king of numbers is more than the king of strength – HAUSA

The little fellow does what he can; the big fellow does what he wants – HAITIAN

What Power did, Hate cannot undo – UGANDAN

When the lion roars all the animals are quiet – SWAHILI

If there is a big tree, there are small trees in its shade – MAMPRUSSI

It is the chief's servant that causes people to fear the chief – TSHI

PRACTICALITY

[The] maggot that is found in...meat is meat also – IGBO

A person scratches herself where she can touch – HAYA

Bad water also quenches the fire – MAMPRUSSI

Hang your knapsack where you can reach it – HAITIAN

If you ask for a hen, first make sure there is one scratching nearby – UGANDAN

It (the river) is crossed where it is shallow – KIKUYU

Running on a roof ends at the edge of it – SWAHILI

The hunter does not shoot what he does not see – IGBO

The spear you have, throw – UGANDAN

You kill a snake with the club that you have in your hand – EWE

PRAISE

Avoid those who always praise you – SWAHILI

If a child is at work and you praise her, she will get strength to do the same again – MAMPRUSSI

Praise is due to those who have merits – SWAHILI

Praise people to encourage people to do more – YORUBA

When a gift is praised, it will beget another gift – IGBO

PREMATURENESS

Before you kill an animal, do not imagine what its skin will make – HAYA

Do not buy a carry-cloth before the baby is born – TSWANA

Do not laugh at the fallen; there may be slippery places ahead – TSWANA

Do not measure a tree that is still growing – MALAGASY

Don't ever count the eggs in the hen's belly – HAITIAN

Food is not rejected while still under cover – IGBO

Hol' de cow befo' you bargain fo' sell de beef – GUYANAN
Hold/have the cow before you bargain to sell the beef.

How can you manage to swallow before you have bitten? – NYANJA

Laugh at the end – SWAHILI

Nebber [never] t[h]row [a]way dutty [dirty] water befo'[re] you hab [have] clean – JAMAICAN

The animal is not dead yet and [yet] you say, 'I add its tail to my charms.' – GANDA

The razor-blade you have not shaved with yet, you praise for its sharp edge – GANDA

PREPAREDNESS

A dog isn't reared on the day one travels [into] the bush [to hunt] – MAMPRUSSI

A mouse that has two holes will not die – GURAGE

A stick which is far away cannot help you kill a snake – TSONGA

Carry a weapon always, one day it will be useful to you – SWAHILI

Don't join in a fight if you have no weapons – SWAHILI

Having spears, have two; when one misses the other one strikes – SHONA

She who knows a matter beforehand confuses the liar – YORUBA

It is not the day on which the yam is planted that we fix sticks for its climbers – TSHI

It is the one who has locked his house that goes on a journey – SHONA

Left hand, learn before the right one is broken – OVAMBO

One does not make a shield on the battlefield – AFRICAN

Preparing yourself early is better than curing yourself when it reaches you – MAMPRUSSI

Readiness has no fears – TWI

Some hope for rain even though they have not prepared their fields – KIKUYU

That which comes when you know of it robs you of little – UGANDAN

The person who is ever ready for war is never defeated – EWE

The stick can't be called when needed – SUKUMA

The stick which is at your friend's house will not drive away the leopard – GANDA

To mediate in a fight, go with a shield – LUYIA

Walk with a stick when the person ahead of you slips – SWAHILI

You cannot make a walking stick on the way – MAASAI

Yuh [you] got to look fuh [for] somewhere to hide before yuh kin [can] steal – BAJAN

A person['s] being prepared beforehand is better than after-reflection – KANURI / BORNU

If you do not learn to shoot, you will not hit your object – OVAMBO

PRESUMPTION

A young monkey does not teach tricks to an old monkey – SWAHILI

Never pack and arrange someone's possessions during her absence because the re-arranging will be hard for you – SHONA

The 'I already know' man doesn't understand anything – MAMPRUSSI

The daughter advised the mother how to deliver a baby – OROMO

The one who can manage a child is the one who has none – SHONA

PRIDE & DIGNITY

'I have taken a shortcut,' says she who has gone astray – UGANDAN

A proud man does not like pride – SWAHILI

If youthful pride were wealth, then every man would have had it in his lifetime – TSHI

One who teaches another person is proud – KAONDE

When a vulture is swept away by a strong wind, he claims he is only playing – KORANKO

A tiger's dignity preserves it when it is asleep – IGBO

 **P**

If donkey bray a[f]ter you, no bray a'ter him – **JAMAICAN**

Though the lion is humbled, he won't play with the pig – **HAUSA**

What is sweet (pleasant) to the senses makes you forget your dignity – **GANDA**

You don't have to turn and look at every dog that barks – **HAITIAN**

PRIORITIES

A great matter puts a smaller out of sight – **YORUBA**

Back can wait, but no[t] belly – **GUYANAN**

Do not consult a wise person in a small matter when a large matter is to hand – **ANCIENT EGYPTIAN**

Fry de big fish fust [first], de lilly [little] one after – **JAMAICAN**

I fried the oil and forgot the onion – **HAUSA**

If food is scarce, start with your own children – **UGANDAN**

If someone goes for water and doesn't return, you don't ask [about] the water pot – **TSHI**

Money that is ransom for your mother you don't give reluctantly – **GANDA**

One whose house is on fire never hunts the rats running from it – **IGBO**

Pull the child out of the water before you punish it – **VAI**

Save your relative from trouble before warning him for having caused the trouble – **IGBO**

Scattered water is better than a broken pitcher – **FULFULDE**

Some pawned themselves to get money – **ANGASS**

The bird whose neck is caught in a trap does not complain of a pain in the neck – **EWE**

The chicken says that she prefers her wing to [be] rotten than her intestine – **IGBO**

The keeping of one's head exceeds the keeping of one's hat – **FULFULDE**

The train does not wait for the passenger – **TSONGA**

Know your problems first before tackling them – IGBO

O lizard on the edge of the pot: smash thee, smash the pot; leave thee, thou spoilest the water – HAUSA

PROGRESSION

Begin in jest and end in earnest – MALAGASY

Does humanity become civilised all at once? – TSHI

The horse-thief started by stealing a fowl – HAUSA

We say one before saying two – TSHI

When they put in the finger, they will also put in the hand: when they have put in the hand, they will also put in the foot – SWAHILI

We help our own children, not our mother's children – TSHI

When two duikers are quarrelling, and they see a lion coming, off they run together, forgetting their quarrel – ASHANTI

You chase the animals away before you advise [i.e. castigate] children – TSHI

You first drive away the hyena and only then ask the goat what made it go in the forest – MAMPRUSSI

You sweep the outside, but the inside is dirty – OVAMBO

PROMISES

A person who took no oath is never guilty of breaking one – IGBO

A promise is a debt and a debt must be paid – SWAHILI

A promise is a debt – SWAHILI

A promise is a man: he who does not keep his promise is not a man – SWAHILI

PROBLEMS

A snake in the bush is easy to fight, but one already in the house becomes a problem – SHONA

If it is entangled I untangle it, and if it comes, I prevent it: 'if it comes I prevent it' is the best – TSHI

If an animal runs quickly, [the] gun will be fired quickly – **IGBO**

PROVERBS

A child asked her mother to teach her proverbs, her mother told her that a thing must happen to necessitate a proverb – **IGBO**

A proverb is the horse of conversation; when the conversation is lost (i.e. flags) a proverb revives it; proverbs and conversation follow each other – **YORUBA**

A wise person who is skilled in the use of proverbs settles disputes – **YORUBA**

One who knows no proverbs knows not their ancestors – **NIGERIAN**

De man dat slow fe promise sure fe keep him wud – **JAMAICAN**
The man that's slow to promise is sure to keep his word.

Hand and tongue never give alike – **ZULU**

She who promises forgets, but she who is waiting remembers – **HAITIAN**

The promise is not the liar, but the one who promises – **KIKUYU**

PROPORTION

A coconut shell full of water is a sea to an ant – **SWAHILI**

A hen pecks what it can swallow – **UGANDAN**

A strong cow's rope is tied to a strong tree – **MAMPRUSSI**

Do not make your weight heavy when your balance is weak – **ANCIENT EGYPTIAN**

Gather firewood to the capacity of the string – **ZULU**

The swearing is out of proportion to what is lost; a needle is lost and an oath is taken upon a god! – **YORUBA**

You don't need an axe to cut up a chicken – **MALAGASY**

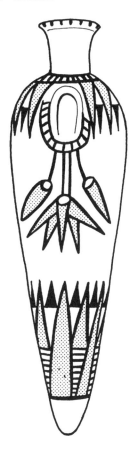

If you tell a proverb to a foolish person, a wise one will understand – TSHI

Not all proverbs are true – HAITIAN

When the occasion comes, the proverb comes – TSHI

PROVOCATION

A snake does not sting someone without cause – OROMO

Ebery [every] day you beat donkey, one day him will kick you – JAMAICAN

He who annoys another only teaches him to strengthen himself – YORUBA

One does not squeeze the tail of a dog to see if it is still sleeping – IGBO

Provocation mek [makes] dummy man talk – JAMAICAN

The truculent person always sports a scar – KIKUYU

PUNISHMENT & LAW

Eating without asking brings dying without being ill – NIGERIAN

If you kyaan't hear, you haffu feel – CREOLE (BELIZE)
If you can't hear you have to feel.

The birch rod doesn't reach the character, but the body will make the connection – NUPE

The body hears better than the ear – HAUSA

The little slap educates – UGANDAN

Dangerous is a man without law in his spirit – TSONGA

Litigation is like a yam hole, no one falls into it and gets out safe and sound – TSHI

Those who do not honour the law praise those who break it – NZIMA

154

Q

If you tap the pot, you see where it is cracked – TSHI

You see an old hen in the market and are anxious to buy it; had it been laying eggs and hatching chicks would the owner have wished to sell it? – YORUBA

QUARRELS & QUARRELLING

Do not quarrel over a matter in which you are wrong – ANCIENT EGYPTIAN

It's on the day when you quarrel that you'll find out the truth – HAITIAN

One who asks 'What did you quarrel about?', renews the quarrel of yesterday – GANDA

Only he who knows the cause of a quarrel knows how to dispute – HO

The quarrel of the sheep doesn't concern the goats – HO

Those who quarrel are those who make up – SWAHILI

To quarrel about things which do not belong to you, is to shed tears for nothing – GANDA

When you quarrel wid [with] you fren' [friend], den [then] you know how much dem [them] know [a]'bout you – JAMAICAN

Without a second person, a quarrel cannot start – SWAHILI

Running away does not end a dispute – GANDA

Seeking quarrels is easy; it's holding up your arguments that's difficult – HAITIAN

QUALITY

A bad thing is sold cheaply – TWI

A good thing brings theft upon you – GANDA

A good thing sells itself; a bad thing wants advertising – SWAHILI

Bad t[h]ing no hab [have] owner – JAMAICAN

The good item always has a willing buyer – KIKUYU

What is good is good: milk is not savoured with salt – SHONA

A person who bombards you with questions makes you speak about something you wanted to hide – GANDA

A question is not an accusation – GANDA

Asking is not stupidity – UGANDAN

Asking questions will enable one to find the right answer – MENDE

Don't go without questioning – SWAHILI

No one is without knowledge except him who asks no questions – FULFULDE

One who did not ask (what kind of food) ate the flesh of the dead – SWAHILI

The child who asks questions dies a redoubtable man – FIPA

Silence finishes the argument – GANDA

The man overwhelmed by another's arguments does not return to discuss matters – KIKUYU

The quiet one puts an end to an argument – OVAMBO

Tap [stop] quarrel before fight come – JAMAICAN

QUESTIONING

A man with a mouth cannot go astray – SOUTHERN AFRICA

The one who asks for the path will not lose the way – KIKUYU

To ask is not foolishness, it is the desire to hear fully – LOZI

To ask is to know – UGANDAN

Examine long; be in the right long – MALAGASY

If a matter be dark, dive to the bottom – YORUBA

If you haven't measured the water you don't know that it is deep – MAMPRUSSI

You cannot tell the contents of a parcel until you open it – NIGERIAN

R

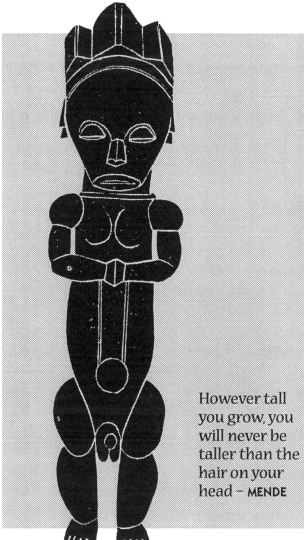

No matter how much you turn around, your heels will always be behind you – IGBO

Spy on the mountain beats one on the plain – FIPA

The breaking of wind by the headman is blamed on the commoner – ZULU

The shoulders are not higher than the head – KAONDE

When a man of noble family is mad, people say he is only drunk – TSHI

When a senior one blunders, a junior person is punished – SWAHILI

When two big bottle deh [there] a-table [on the table], little wan [one] no bu'[s]iness – GUYANAN

However tall you grow, you will never be taller than the hair on your head – MENDE

RANK

A child is never old before its parents – SWAHILI

As one's rank, so they give seat – IGBO

Be the neck never so, long the head is on top – HAUSA

Kings may grow beards as they do not have to blow the fire – NIGERIAN

REASON

She who does not recognise reason is not told the reason – SWAHILI

There must be a reason for the person who hastens off into the desert; if something is not running after her, she is running after something – YORUBA

When the rain falls at night and you do not hear it, don't you see from the ground the next day? – TSHI

When yuh see a man fishin' in a dry pond, he does know what [h]'e['s] doin' – BAJAN

When the tree plays with the wind, it loses its leaves – HAITIAN

When you show a monkey how to throw stones, it will break your head first – HAITIAN

REDUNDANCY

Blind man need no lookin'-glass – JAMAICAN

If you hab darg fe bark fe you, no need fe you fe bark – JAMAICAN
If you have a dog to bark for you, there's no need for you to bark yourself.

The child that isn't crying has no need to be nursed – HAITIAN

Trying to daub red ochre on a redbuck – TSWANA

RECKLESSNESS

'Come what may' causes the destruction of a country – TSHI

[The] animal who follows the monkey may break [its] leg – IGBO

A chicken who is drunk has never seen a fox who is mad – IGBO

A rat that plays around a trap is looking for death – IGBO

He who throws a stone into a crowd does not know who will be hit – SWAHILI

He who throws stones in the night kills his brother – EWE

If you haven't crossed a river, you don't insult the crocodile for its long mouth – MAMPRUSSI

The butterfly that flies against the thorn will soon have its wings torn – YORUBA

What the crocodile eats, finds it in deep waters – KAONDE

REGRET & REPENTANCE

'If only I knew' comes after the act – LUYIA

Doing one's best drives away regret – MALAGASY

Departure does not prevent a person from returning – KIKUYU

He who has not repented has not seen evil – MONGO

If a stupid man repents he becomes a wise man – ANCIENT EGYPTIAN

It is better to spend the night in the irritation of the offence than in repentance for the revenge – TAMASHEK

Repentance is deeds – SWAHILI

RELATIONSHIP & RELATIVES

If your relative does not collude, it is difficult for outsiders to plan your assassination – YORUBA

Kinship cannot be washed with water and removed – SHONA

One who says "somewhere is far away" has no relationship with anyone there – SWAHILI

Relationship is a half measure which is filled by being given food – SHONA

Relationship is a matter of visits – ANGASS

The uncle to one brother is uncle to all of you – MAMPRUSSI

Whatever you have secured eat with relatives; a stranger forgets – SHONA

Why should I dislike you, am I your relative? – FULANI

Yuh [you] look like yuh livin' at yuh [your] aunt['s].[i.e. malnourished] – BAJAN

It is useless for me to recognise one who does not recognise me – SWAHILI

Far-off [a]gree best – BAJAN

They who leave one another forget one another – KIKUYU

RELIGION

Christian forgib [forgive] freely an'[d] forget freely – JAMAICAN

The fetish priest who says it will rain and the fetish priest who says it will not rain, they are all lying fetish priests – TSHI

Christian life is in the heart of man, not in his words – TSHWA

Pr'yer in de mout' only is no pr'yer – JAMAICAN
Prayer in the mouth only is no prayer.

Pr'yer needn't be long when fait'[h] [s]'trong – JAMAICAN

God help me!: you have a right to pray so if you also exert yourself – GANDA

REPUTATION

A bad name kills its owner – UGANDAN

A daring man can get convicted for what he did not commit – HAYA

A dog which steals leaves its puppies a bad name – KAONDE

A drop can cause a stain that a bucketful of water cannot remove – SWAHILI

A good name is better than riches – TSHI

A good name protects you from the shameless – UGANDAN

A good name shines in the dark – SWAHILI

A man dies but his tongue [his words/ideas] does not rot – TWI

A person takes her name with her wherever whe goes – TSHI

Do not handle mud when there is no water – SHONA

Don't dress me in a dog's skin: the leopard might eat me – UGANDAN

Every person has a name – OVAMBO

For one day a person may behave disgracefully, then for all his life he is put to shame – YORUBA

He who is wont to provoke others is called a provoker even when he is provoked – KIKUYU

If a goat barks at a stranger, it's to the dog's shame – MAMPRUSSI

If a man is detected in a dishonest transaction, never again will he be employed – ANCIENT EGYPTIAN

If the spirit world possesses nothing else, it has at least the power of its name – ASHANTI

If you are always trustworthy and you tell a lie, it isn't noticed – TSHI

If you live in a bad town, you are disgraced – TSHI

Leave a good name behind in case you return – GOGO

The dead person is abused – OVAMBO

The river may be dried up but its name is never forgotten – IGBO

The thief who doesn't get caught passes off as an honourable person – HAITIAN

The tortoise was setting out on a journey and someone asked her when she would be back. 'When I have lost my reputation,' she answered – **YORUBA**

To disgrace a hero is worse than to kill him – **IGBO**

We take a good name away from a strange country; we do not carry a good name into a strange country – **JABO**

When a liar tells the truth, no one believes him – **HAITIAN**

When yuh [you] know de [the] cat does steal butter yuh always blame [h]'im – **BAJAN**

You should not be surprised to smell badly if you have decayed – **SWAHILI**

If a doctor is mistaken he leaves by the back of the house – **IGBO**

One loses one's reputation in one day, but the disgrace is for all days – **YORUBA**

There is nothing as painful as being disgraced – **TSHI**

RESPECT & DISRESPECT

'Father, stop and let me tell you what you ought to do,' it is not permitted to speak so – **ASHANTI**

A child who has no respect for his own mother cannot respect someone else's mother – **LUYIA**

Familiarity breeds contempt: distance secures respect – **YORUBA**

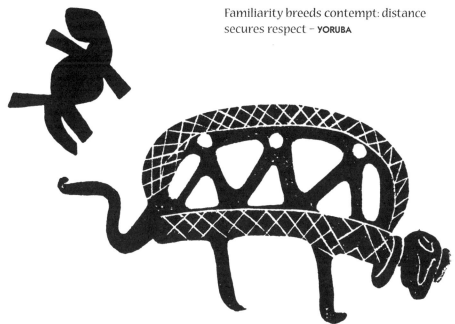

RESPONSIBILITY

A person has to die for what he has done – SHONA

One should not invite a curse and leave it to another to bear – TWI

As you threw the knife (and it tore the hide) now look for the needle (and sew it again) – UGANDAN

Bruk [break] calabash, bring new one – JAMAICAN

Bull horn nebber too heaby fe bull head – JAMAICAN
The bull's horns are never too heavy for the bull's head.

Do not hurt yourself then turn round and say: "they have bewitched me" – TSWANA

He who stole the food does not cease denying the theft – MONGO

If two slaves look after a cow, it dies of starvation – TSHI

If your part of the battlefield is in a difficult situation, you don't leave it and go to where it is easy – TSHI

It is the fowl with chicks that flees from the hawk – HAUSA

One who kicks a dog aims at its owner – UGANDAN

He who thinks little of you calls you while you are eating – UGANDAN

If you are supported by someone, you respect him – TSHI

No one shakes hands with Ampoforo (a leper) out of respect for her – TSHI

One who does not value you cheats you – HAYA

One who makes faces at you behind your back respects you – GANDA

Receiving honour won't make you a noble, and giving honour won't make you a slave, so it is well to honour one another – MALAGASY

Respect must be paid on both sides – ZULU

Walking on another's property means being mild – LAMBA

Once you have crossed the river you can be rude to the crocodile – TWI

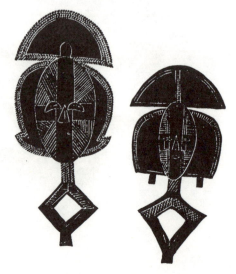

The fault is with the son, the father is blameless – ZULU

The man who thrust his hand into the bag knows what he took out – IDOMA

[The] one who borrows is the one who pays back – HAYA

The one who puts the iron in the fire is the one [who] removes it – UGANDAN

The thing responsible for the pregnancy, the same is responsible for the child – MAMPRUSSI

The weight of the problem is felt by the owner – GUSII

Those who blow on the fire will run from the smoke – MAMPRUSSI

When a man who has many wives is sick, he dies of starvation – TSHI

When li'[tt]l[e] boy put on big man trouse[r]s, wha'[t] he get he mus'[t] take – GUYANAN

You blame the wolf even though the goats are wandering in the meadow at night – OVAMBO

Those who keep stolen things for robbers encourage robbery – YORUBA

When a boy reaches ten years old there are no more excuses – FIPA

Once the bee settles in the honeycomb, it starts to make the honey – KIKUYU

The mouth which ate the seeds is also the same one that asks what it will plant – KIKUYU

Whether the package on sale yields profit or not to the owner, the carrier's wages will be completely paid – NIGERIAN

REVELATION

A secret shared between two people ceases to be a secret – HAYA

A thief steals by night; he is found by day – ANCIENT EGYPTIAN

A woman hides the penis; she won't hide the belly – MAMPRUSSI

R

He who cultivates in secret is betrayed by the smoke – CHAGGA

Ti[h]ef man no like moon – GUYANAN

To hide a sick person is to be finally betrayed by groans – SUKUMA

What is in one's heart is no evidence – KIKUYU

When the lifter lifts the stone then what is under comes out – EWE

When the sharing is hand by hand, the one who is loved will be known – IGBO

People know about the person who speaks, not the one who is quiet – OVAMBO

REVENGE & RETRIBUTION

He who makes you shed tears: you make him shed blood – GANDA

Kiss (ass) till you could kick (ass) – CREOLE (BELIZE)

Revenge is not wickedness – IGBO

Silliness is not revenged – SWAHILI

The first vengeance is insignificant in comparison with the last – YORUBA

The sound of the gun that killed my brother burns in my ears – JABO

To eat an alligator is not gluttony, it is simply a matter of tit for tat – TEMNE

To forget a wrong is the best revenge – SWAHILI

R

To take revenge is often to sacrifice oneself
– **KONGO**

REWARD

As a person spreads his mat, so he will lie
on it – **YORUBA**

She who deserves wine should not be given
water – **TSHI**

One who searches finds – **GANDA**

If you sow falsehood, you reap deceit – **TWI**

It is far where there is nothing; where
there is something you are determined to
reach – **SHONA**

One gets a reward of what one has done;
he who passes excreta on the road will
encounter many flies on his return –
YORUBA

The rat says, 'Put plenty of food in the trap,'
for...he risks his neck – **EFIK**

RIVALS & RIVALRY

A courtier does not mourn his dead
companion – **OVAMBO**

A woman who has lost her rival has no
sorrow – **WOLOF**

If two friends flirt with one woman, it
doesn't take long before a fight begins –
TSHI

The speed of the rabbit is because there is
no good dog – **KAONDE**

The tortoise's competitors are snails –
MAMPRUSSI

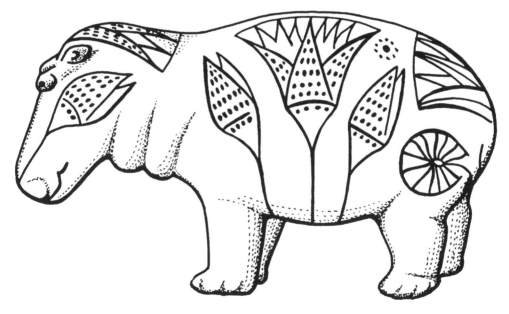

 **R**

Two cap'n can't 'teer wan ship – GUYANAN
Two captains can't steer one ship.

Two dogs after a bone are never in agreement – HAITIAN

Two kings do not rule in one town – EWE

Two smart rats can'[t] live in one hole – BAJAN

RULERS

A king is a king because of people – ZULU

A man from the wilderness is not made [a] courtier; he would destroy the country – OVAMBO

A good chief is like a well: as soon as it caves in the people will discover how much water they need – NAMIBIAN

No person responsible for the affairs of the state is a child – TSHI

Other people's wisdom prevents a chief from being called a fool – IGBO

The maker of the king doesn't rule with him – NDEBELE

A blow to the head of a ruler is forbidden, but not a word – AFRICAN

S

Because lizard no good fe eat, him no 'fraid fe walk a road – JAMAICAN
Because the lizard is no good to eat he is not afraid to walk on the road.

SAFETY

'Tak kyar,' de mudda ob safety – JAMAICAN
'Take care,' is the mother of safety.

If you get a good place to stand, you make fun of the cobra – TSHI

Whatever compels an orang-utan to climb a tree hurriedly will no longer be there before it ever comes down again – YORUBA

When the crab flees, it runs into the ocean – TSHI

SAMENESS

A man who is always crying is not listened to – NANDI

Black will not laugh at black – OVAMBO

De [the] mornin' and de evenin' is de same day – BAJAN

Don't run from the smoke into the fire – TEMNE

He fled from the sword and hid in the scabbard (into which the sword will return) – YORUBA

If you were no good yesterday, you're no better today – HAITIAN

It is all one whether [a person] is bitten by an old snake or by its offspring: both are poisonous – NANDI

One corpse cannot laugh at another – MONGO

There is no difference between a thief and his accomplice – KIKUYU

SATISFACTION

A man who eats what he has, his desire is for what he has not – IGBO

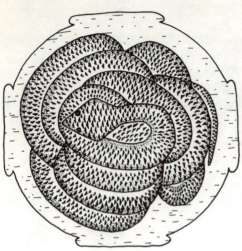

He who makes love to a married woman is killed on her doorstep – ANCIENT EGYPTIAN

Tell a child to call anybody he knows, he will call his mother's boyfriend – IGBO

SECRETS & SECRECY

A matter between two persons is not a matter for three people – ACHOLI

He who hides his illness, will be hidden by his illness – IGBO

If you haven't lifted your arm above, no one will know you grow hair – MAMPRUSSI

One who is sent with a secret message is not told the meaning of it – SWAHILI

What remains secretly in my heart lets me sleep peacefully at home – HAITIAN

Who comes in secret comes again – SWAHILI

He who is looking for a place to sleep doesn't tell you that he wets the bed – TSHI

A satisfied person throws a spear at God – OROMO

He who has had his fill becomes thoughtless – KIKUYU

She who is sated spits out honey – GALLA

If you buy something and have to sweat before you pay for it, then you are pleased with yourself – TSHI

The one who has bread to eat...does not appreciate the severity of a famine – YORUBA

The satisfied despise the gift – UGANDAN

To look for a fly in your food means that you have had enough – PEDI

When a child has eaten that which kept him awake, he will sleep – IGBO

When the cat's belly is full, he says that the rat's tail is bitter – HAITIAN

SCANDAL & CORRUPTION

Scandal is like an egg: when it is hatched it has wings – MALAGASY

A hog that has wallowed in the mud seeks a clean person to rub against – YORUBA

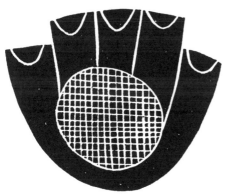

SELF

'It belongs to me' is better than 'it belongs to us.' – FULFULDE

A man's greatness and respect come from himself – SWAHILI

Before healing others, heal thyself – WOLOF

She who advises herself meets no hatred – KIKUYU

Ho' on to weh you have an grab fo' mo' – CREOLE (BELIZE)
Hold on to what you have and grab for more.

In doing good one does it to oneself; in doing evil one does it to oneself – TAMASHEK

Nebber pull out you inside fe gi' 'tranger and den tek trash fe 'tuff yourself – JAMAICAN
Never pull out your guts to give to a stranger and then take rubbish to stuff yourself.

Nobody cracks palm kernels with their own teeth for their neighbour – TSHI

Our having is better than their having – MAMPRUSSI

The dog with the bone has no friends - and isn't looking for any – HAITIAN

The ordering is finished: there's nobody left to send up but yourself – SUKUMA

Thirst cannot be quenched by proxy – MONGO

Water which you pour on yourself does not chill you – IGBO

When a bachelor lies that he has a wife, he is deceiving his penis – MAMPRUSSI

Your own saliva does not nauseate you – OVAMBO

One who invites a slap on the cheek will get it – GANDA

SELF-CONTROL

Chieftanship cannot rule itself – SHONA

He who has nobody to tie him up should never go mad – YORUBA

He who turns away from his anger is one who is far from the anger of the god – ANCIENT EGYPTIAN

The great praise of a wise woman is self-control in her manner of life – ANCIENT EGYPTIAN

To control yourself is greater than if they control you – MAMPRUSSI

When you are given a drum to carry, it does not mean you should play it – SHONA

 **S**

SELF-CRITICISM

He gave a sermon and forgot himself –
SWAHILI

She who has eyes watches himself first –
UGANDAN

My eyes, look at me too – OVAMBO

When it threatens to rain, the man whose
roof leaks blames himself – KURIA

You cannot point an accusing finger
without leaving four directed at yourself –
IGBO

SELF-DECEPTION

A lame man said the load on his head was
not properly balanced, and was told "Its
unevenness began from the ground." –
YORUBA

Every one's character is good in their own
eyes – YORUBA

He gave you some but added to it in his
mind – OVAMBO

She who looks at another's field sees many
more weeds than does its owner – KIKUYU

That which is sweet to the dog is apt to kill
the dog – IGBO

The baboons laugh at each other's
foreheads – ZULU

The king's dog thinks that they bow to it
because of its bark – UGANDAN

The person whom one loves can never be
seen to misbehave – YORUBA

Do not set your heart on the property of
another, saying, I will live thereon; acquire
property yourself – ANCIENT EGYPTIAN

Giving to oneself is better than receiving –
OVAMBO

God saith, 'Guard thyself, and I will guard
thee.' – SWAHILI

Insects follow [i.e. make use of] a log to
cross a river – IGBO

It is no good asking the spirits to help you
run if you don't mean to sprint – GANDA

The axe of the stranger cannot finish your
work – SWAHILI

The hyena said: 'It is not only that I have
luck, but my leg is strong.' – MAASAI

SELF-HELP

'Save me' is a slow deliverance; help yourself
– TSWANA

A mouth does not eat on behalf of another
– SHONA

SELF-INTEREST

A man does not go to his wife with another
man more handsome than himself – IGBO

A person who is feeling cold does not need
to be shown the fire – LUYIA

S

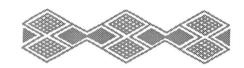

Don't throw stones where you keep bottles
– **TEMNE**

He who fights for a head, fights for his own head – **SHONA**

I'm not going to lend you a stick to break my head with – **LOUISIANA** CREOLE

If a young person accepts an errand she includes her own – **SHONA**

If one does not know how to publicize himself over the vanquished, the vanquished will publicize itself over him – **IGBO**

It is the place one lives in that one repairs – **IGBO**

No set hungry duck fe [to] watch carn [corn] – **JAMAICAN**

Nobody forces the monkey to eat the fruit of the tamarind tree – **TSHI**

The animal standing does not wait for another lying down – **SHONA**

The death of the sergeant is good for the corporal – **HAITIAN**

The person in hiding does not cough – **TWI**

The sheep is never declared guiltless at the court of the leopard – **EWE**

The well where you draw water you never make dirty – **SWAHILI**

Wash you' own face befo' you wash you' matty wan – **GUYANAN**
Wash your own face before you wash your friend's own.

What sort of kindness should that be if a cat induces a rat to come and play? – **SHONA**

When one has just sufficient money for one's own needs, one does not let it out as a loan – **TSHI**

SELF-KNOWLEDGE

Don't heng yuh hat weh yuh can' reach um – **BAJAN**
Don't hang your hat where you can't reach it.

Drunk man nebba [never] know he drunk – **GUYANAN**

If the ox knew his strength, he would never let anyone lasso him – **HAITIAN**

Know thyself better than he does who speaks of thee – **WOLOF**

Lack of self-knowledge makes one a slave – **EWE**

Look into yourself – **OVAMBO**

Man know he weak, he refuse 'trang [strong] man['s] challenge – **GUYANAN**

The eye that sees, sees not itself – **ETSAKO**

"To despise one's equal is to despise oneself – **EWE**

What is in the heart, the heart alone knows – **FIPA**

When your eye shows you other people's immorality, say: "Eye, those people have eyes too." – **SWAHILI**

SELF-LOVE & SELF-INJURY

A man's ways are good in his own eyes – **JABO**

Supporting someone doesn't mean neglecting oneself – **MAMPRUSSI**

The one who judges himself calls himself handsome – **KIKUYU**

Wounds other than yours stink – **SHONA**

A person who harms himself should not cry for pity from anybody – **SWAHILI**

He cut a tree and fell over it himself – **GA**

I have exposed myself to laughter, and I say they shouldn't laugh at me – **TSHI**

One's enemy is one's own self – **ZULU**

You were the one who started the fire, now the smoke is in your eyes – **SWAHILI**

SELF-RELIANCE

'Become self-dependent' is not an insult – **TSHI**

'Come back quickly' is not as good as going and getting it yourself – **TSHI**

A horse brings you to the battlefield but it does not fight – **GURAGE**

An only child struggles alone when faced with problems – **GUSII**

 **S**

By sending someone to fetch his tail, the rock rabbit failed to get one – **SHONA**

Each firefly lights its own way – **HAITIAN**

One who goes herself to buy things carries them too – **KIKUYU**

He who has no child must get his legs to do his errands – **LUYIA**

She who looks after her own business has no trouble – **KIKUYU**

The work is done if one does it – **KIKUYU**

Don't be indiscreet and then expect another to be discreet – **OROMO**

If one quarrels with corn, hunger will kill them – **HAUSA**

If you quarrel with the high-road, which way will you go? – **HAITIAN**

The hungry person will not laugh when the server of food breaks wind – **FULANI**

The person for whom the interpretation is being done has to rely on the interpreter – **KIKUYU**

You see eberybody [everybody] run, tek [take] time – **JAMAICAN**

SELF-RESPECT

A useless task is only fit for a dog, and the dog when he sees it is useless will leave it – **HAUSA**

If someone doesn't like themself, you shouldn't tell them to like you – **MAMPRUSSI**

If you are honoured, do not dishonour yourself – **TWI**

Mek youself floor-claat, pipple wipe dem foot 'pan you – **CREOLE (BELIZE)**
Make a floor-cloth of yourself and people will wipe their feet upon you.

The chameleon says that others respect you if you respect yourself, and that is why it walks like a king – **EWE**

When a lion allows himself to be put on a chain it is no disgrace for it to stay there – **AMHARIC**

Beg man fo' wo'k, but na beg am fo' eat – **GUYANAN**
Beg a man for work, but don't beg from him to eat.

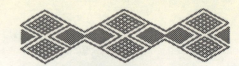

SELFISHNESS

He acts like a dog who drives the flies away from food it has spurned – JABO

Let my cow die here rather than give birth in your place – UGANDAN

The one who entered first closes the door on the rest – OROMO

When I find hard work to do, I call my friends to help me; but when I find a well-salted eel, I find I don't need help – MALAGASY

When I remember it I laugh, because it is not I who am concerned – GANDA

You are bad, if you're only good for yourself – HAITIAN

SEQUENCE

A child one does not instruct on return: one instructs him when going – LAMBA

Choose your neighbour before you buy your house – HAUSA

Do not swallow before you chew – SHONA

Whenever you want to carry something heavy, you rest it first on the knee for it to reach the head – MAMPRUSSI

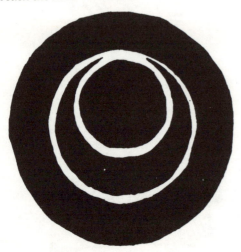

SERVICE

A little service out of friendship is worth more than a great service which is forced – GANDA

A tailor does not choose the cloth – SWAHILI

I serve you, but that doesn't make me a dog – HAITIAN

If you don't do the important thing for a person, all the little things you did won't count – HAITIAN

Serve a wise man, that he may serve you – ANCIENT EGYPTIAN

To serve now does not prevent one from being served in the future – KIKUYU

SHAME

Being embarrassed is beginning to become ashamed – HAITIAN

Nobody is twice ashamed – GA

Of the two, shame and death, death is preferable – TSHI

There is nothing that hurts like shame – ASHANTI

S

The great are open to shame, and the small are open to fear – MALAGASY

The great are open to shame, and the small are open to fear – MALAGASY

SHARING

God gave you, to give to me – AMHARIC

It is not difficult to share two things – EWE

'Ours' is not 'mine.' – SWAHILI

People who share with others are seldom hungry – HAITIAN

Put it down, let us divide it; things fought over get spoiled – LAMBA

Something small is not divided – OVAMBO

One who has not carried your burden knows not what it weighs – HAYA

It is one man who kills the elephant but the whole town eats it – TSHI

SICKNESS

A sick man despises not medicine – HAUSA

Disease does not go under any other name than 'Conceal me and I cause your death.' – YORUBA

If you have no time to attend to your illness, you get time to die – TWI

Illness enters the body with less difficulty than it meets on going away – KIKUYU

One day's fever takes away the health of the whole year – SWAHILI

Sick people are like kings – MALAGASY

Sickness ride harse [horse] come, him tek [take] foot go [a]'way – JAMAICAN

The illness that gave notice, does not kill the patient – IGBO

SIGHT & SEEING

Belieb [believe] half what you see - nuttin' what you hear – JAMAICAN

De [the] more you look, de less you see – JAMAICAN

Eyes have no boundary – SHONA

He who does not see by himself, does not see even when it is shown to him – SWAHILI

I believe when I see – IGBO

It is through your eyes that you hear what is being said – TSHI

'Tan [stand] far, see better – JAMAICAN

The eye discerns the beauty but not the kindness of a person – KIKUYU

The man who looks in front of him does not stumble and fall – ANCIENT EGYPTIAN

To hear is not like seeing with one's own eyes – TSWANA

What the eyes don't see never hurts the heart – MARTINIQUE

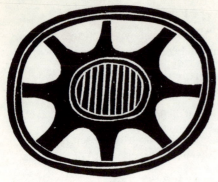

SILENCE

'Can't speak' isn't without anger – MAMPRUSSI

'Know and keep quiet' means 'understand and will not say.' – MAMPRUSSI

If 'peech wut a shillin', silence wut a poun' – JAMAICAN
If speech is worth a shilling, silence is worth a pound.

If you don't know anything about a town, you don't tell anything about it – TSHI

One who talks, thinks: but one who keeps silent, thinks more – GANDA

Silence conceals foolishness – ANCIENT EGYPTIAN

Silence ends disputes – UGANDAN

Silence is also speech – FULFULDE

Silence itself is eloquent – FULANI

Still tongue keep wise head – GUYANAN

The eyes are for seeing, the ears for hearing, and the lips to shut up – HAITIAN

To know and keep quiet is wickedness – MAMPRUSSI

When you see something, if you do not say something, you will not suffer something – SWAHILI

Yeye mus' see and aise mus' hear but mout' mus' shut – JAMAICAN
Eye must see and ears must see but mouth must keep shut.

SIN & WRONGDOING

If you don't confess your sins, you can't be forgiven – HAITIAN

Sin devours the one who has committed it – SHONA

The redeemer of sin is confession – TSONGA

The reward of sin is death – SHONA

It is best to let an offence repeat itself at least three times: the first may be an accident; the second a mistake; but the third is likely to be intentional – KONGO

Many are cursed for the crime of one – OVAMBO

Nobody is twice ashamed – GA

The wrongdoer forgets, but not the wronged – BONDEI

When you touch what doesn't belong to you, you're in the wrong – HAITIAN

Wrongdoing is a hill: you walk on your own and observe that of another – HAUSA

 **S**

A newly committed crime or mistake awakens sleeping ones – BEMBA

If you see wrong-doing and say nothing about it, it may come to you later – TSHI

SLAVERY

A new slave: give him a cloth that he may forget (or deny) the land of his birth – SWAHILI

A slave knows his master – TSHI

Even a slave has once been somebody's child – SWAHILI

SLEEP

Big blanket mek [make] man sleep late – JAMAICAN

Even the cleverest child cannot escape sleep – SWAHILI

Sleep is death's little brother – HAITIAN

Sleep knows no misery – HAITIAN

Sleep, the near relative of death – TSWANA

SLOWNESS

Daddy tortoise goes slow; but he gets to the goal while Daddy Deer is asleep – LOUISIANA

Go slowly so you may arrive safely – SWAHILI

Going slowly doesn't stop one arriving – FULFULDE

Rather take a long route and be confident of reaching your destination – LUYIA

Slow and sure – IGBO

Slowness is sometimes more advantageous than speed – TSHI

Thorns pierce slowly if a man goes slowly – OROMO

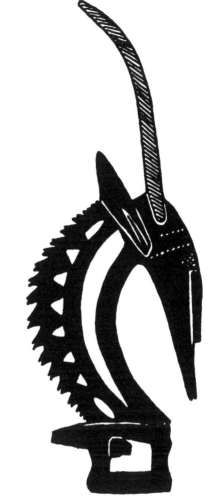

You are in no hurry: like a bald man fetching his razor – GANDA

The turtle says: 'quickness is a good thing, and slowness is also a good thing.' – TSHI

SOLUTION(S)

Every door has its own key – SWAHILI

Get into the mud, water will remove it; get into dispute, the mouth will get you out of it; be overtaken by sorrow, you can appeal to your friends – MALAGASY

S

He has seen the way to climb up; but the way to climb down he does not see – GANDA

'If you are solving a problem and don't know how to solve it, then that is the solution – TSHI

Noisy talk does not bring about a solution – OVAMBO

SOUR GRAPES

An ugly person comforts himself by saying that pretty is vanity – IGBO

If you can't buy, you say it is not delicious – TSHI

The antelope which keeps a long way off has tough meat on it – UGANDAN

The monkey who dropped [a] kola nut accidentally said it was a present to the earth and its people – YORUBA

The mouse will rather destroy the beans than be unable to eat [them] – YORUBA

When you cannot get what you wish for, you despise it, or those who have it – HAYA

When you do not know how to dance, then you say, 'The drum is not sounding sweetly.' – ASHANTI

SPEECH & TALKING

A thoughtless man is known by his speech – OVAMBO

A word fallen on the ground [i.e. spoken] is left to be picked up by others – KIKUYU

Be haste [hasty] fe [to] listen, but slow fe talk – JAMAICAN

Be patient when you speak, and you will say distinguished things – ANCIENT EGYPTIAN

Don't open your mouth before you think – MARAKWET

'Fish get ketch by e mout' – CREOLE (BELIZE)
The fish gets caught by his mouth.

He who falls by his foot (i.e. slips) shall rise again; he who falls by his mouth shall not rise – EFIK

If yeye [eye] no see, mout'[h] can't talk – GUYANAN

If you check your tongue you will spare your whole body – UGANDAN

If you no hab [have] good fe [to] say, no say bad – JAMAICAN

Is de ansah [answer] does bring de row – GUYANAN

'Isn't the king fat?,' says the one with nothing to say – UGANDAN

No fly can settle on his mouth. [talkativeness] – NDEBELE

One who talks too much is a revealer of secrets – IGBO

Padlock you'[r] tongue, or it lock you up – GUYANAN

Rain covers footprints but never what was spoken with the tongue – IGBO

Sleep on it before speaking.. – ANCIENT EGYPTIAN

Stupidity is in the mouth – OVAMBO

Sweet tongue hide bad heart – JAMAICAN

Talking is loving one another – KIKUYU

Talking is not doing – IGBO

The less they think, the more they talk – HAITIAN

Answer not a man when he is wroth, but remove thyself from him – AFRICAN

Speak gently to him that hath spoken in anger, for soft words are the medicine for his heart – ANCIENT EGYPTIAN

The mouth entraps – LAMBA

The mouth is easy to open (but) difficult to close – SHONA

The mouth talks plenty that the heart does not say – EWE

The mouth that spoke ill will eventually speak good – IGBO

The rod does not hurt, it is the mouth that hurts – TSONGA

The talkative disclose their father's defect – UGANDAN

The talkative person reveals things about himself – TSHI

The tongue is a good cudgel – HAITIAN

The way one speaks is the way one acts – UGANDAN

 **S**

The word invites you to stay the night, but the countenance sends you home again the same day – MALAGASY

Think first before you speak – TSONGA

Wha'[t] yeye [eye] no see, mout' can'[t] talk – JAMAICAN

What you say is what you will be judged by – LUYIA

When high words confuse the talk, low words will untangle it – JABO

You catch cow by him horn, but man by him wud [word] – JAMAICAN

You know what to say, but not what you will be told – MAASAI

Your tongue is your enemy – MALAGASY

Yuh can' prevent yuh ear from hearin' but yuh kin stop yuh mout' from talkin.' – BAJAN
You can't prevent your ear from hearing but you can stop your mouth from talking.

Conversation is like dry meat: its savour abides – BONDEI

Conversation is the food of the ears – TRINIDADIAN

Conversation finishes anger – SUKUMA

If you are greedy in conversation, you lose the wisdom of your friend – TSHI

Talk a de aise food – JAMAICAN
Talk is the ears' food.

If the elders leave you a legacy of dignified language, you do not abandon it and speak childish language – TSHI

One's own language is never hard – IGBO

SPIRIT

Parents give birth to the body, not to the soul – UGANDAN

The soul does not grow old; it does not grow grey hair – GANDA

Your foot is sick, but that which ties you together (soul) is well – SUKUMA

STRANGERS

A stranger does not know when there is danger – IGBO

A stranger is blind even though she has eyes – HAUSA

A stranger knows the secret: a village child has revealed [it] – MAMPRUSSI

A strong man's club is tested by foreigners – KIKUYU

The eyes of the stranger may be very large, but he does not see the inner things of the town or nation – GA

Where relatives fight, a stranger should keep aloof – SHONA

 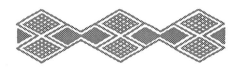
STUBBORNNESS

A person who does not hear, learns when the axe is in his head – NYANJA

He who doesn't wish to be told will not be told – SUKUMA

He who refutes those who advise him won't refute those who bury him – UGANDAN

If you refuse to be made straight when you are green, you will not be made straight when you become dry – KAMBA

The ear that pays no heed to advice is usually cut off with the head – NIGERIAN

The obstinate die in obstinacy – ZULU

The stubbornness of the spider: though dead it is still hanging – TEMNE

STUPIDITY

I pointed out to you the moon and all you saw was my finger – SUKUMA

If a stupid man speaks the truth he is not believed – OVAMBO

It is through sheer stupidity and inexperience that a rat challenges a cat to a fight – YORUBA

Respect for a stupid person is stupidity – SWAHILI

Stupidity does not tolerate wisdom – OVAMBO

The stupidity of the goat:to greet the hyena – HAUSA

SUFFERING

Eberybody feel he own pain – GUYANAN

Forgetting is the cure for suffering – SWAHILI

He who has been shaven with (a piece of) bottle can never forget – SWAHILI

Iron is passed through fire to be hardened – SWAHILI

Suffering doesn't kill, it teaches sense – MAMPRUSSI

Suffering makes one disclose what was done in confidence – HAYA

The axe forgets but the cut log does not – SHONA

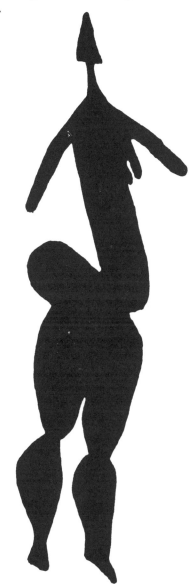

The one who suffers much knows much – **HO**

Those who have never suffered know not the sorrows of others – **HAITIAN**

Time passes, but sufferings leave their scars – **UGANDAN**

SUPERIORITY & INFERIORITY

A one who is stronger than you beats you with your own stick – **GANDA**

A stone is never overturned by the wind – **MONGO**

A straight tree soon leaves the forest – **YORUBA**

A thing that cannot speak obeys the one who can – **GANDA**

A wolf has no cause for apprehension; it is the dog that enters the wolf's den that is in trouble – **YORUBA**

After the elephant there is a still greater animal, the hunter! – **TSHI**

Butter can't fight against the sun – **UGANDAN**

Even if cockroaches come in thousands, one chicken can clear them all – **IGBO**

If the tongue say[s] it be very very long, it cannot vie with the boa constrictor – **GA**

It is the sky that sees the back of the flying bird – **IGBO**

Man you can'[t] beat, you have fe [to] call him you[r] fren' [friend] – **JAMAICAN**

Moon a-run, but day a-ketch am – **GUYANAN**
The moon runs but the day catches him.

The cliffs mock the banks of the river – **KIKUYU**

The dog is a kola nut for the hyena – **HAUSA** [i.e. a titbit]

The elephant makes a dust and the buffalo makes a dust, but the dust of the buffalo is lost in that of the elephant – **YORUBA**

There is no need to quarrel with anybody whose advancement is beyond one's attainment – **YORUBA**

There is no tallness among pigeons: they are all dwarfs – **YORUBA**

When a dog sees a leopard's face it will be silent – **YORUBA**

SUPPORT

A river is enlarged by its tributaries. – **KIKUYU**

Encouragement in warfare is more important than the actual fighting – **IGBO**

S

If the dog has its owner behind it, it will not be afraid of the baboon – **YORUBA**

It's the neck that keeps the head high – **MAMPRUSSI**

One cannot lean upon emptiness – **YORUBA**

The fruit must have a stem before it grows – **JABO**

The goat dwells among men for fear of the leopard – **JABO**

The lamp won't light without a wick – **HAITIAN**

The shrub with one root is not hard to pull up – **HAUSA**

SURPRISE & EXPECTATION

A gun that does not go off leaves its owner in peril – **OVAMBO**

Black fowl can lay white egg.[also: good children can come of bad parents] – **JAMAICAN**

On the hardest rocks, sometimes you'll see beautiful flowers growing – **HAITIAN**

Don't stretch out your open hand to one who has never before given you anything – **UGANDAN**

Good fruit comes from good seed – **TSONGA**

If it is not your turn to prepare a meal and you do it, another person will be thanked for it – **EWE**

It doesn't always rain the way it thunders – **UGANDAN**

Lilly [little] bush sometime'[s] grow betta dan big tree – **JAMAICAN**

Man counts what he is refused, not what he is given – **KIKUYU**

No one removes trouble in order to get trouble – **TSHI**

No tree ever bore fruit without first having flowers – **ASHANTI**

The expected does not arrive – **OVAMBO**

The fruit falls under the tree – **EWE**

SUSPICION

'Tranger nebber walk in a de back door – **JAMAICAN**
A stranger [should] never walk in at the back door.

A mother who is a thief does not trust her daughter – **OROMO**

De [the] fox preach, tek [take] care a [of] de [the] lamb – JAMAICAN

He that hates his neighbour should remember the suspicion he will arouse when misfortune befalls his neighbour – IGBO

If a blind man walks without a walking stick, he is inviting people to question him – SHONA

Just when my sheep got lost, the hyena defecated wool – UGANDAN

No one confesses that they has eaten yam with a knife that is missing – YORUBA

One who is suspected of being a thief should not pick up a young domestic animal to play with it – YORUBA

SWEETNESS

Na eberyt'ing wah gat sugah a-sweet – GUYANAN
Not everything that has sugar is sweet.

Sweet on the lips, sour in the stomach – OVAMBO

Sweetness walks with bitterness – EFIK

There are people who, like sugar cane, are killed for being sweet – KIKUYU

SYMPATHY

A mother will feel pity for a mother – SWAHILI

At the funeral, one cries for the living and not for the dead – IGBO

If Akua stubs her toe we don't sympathise with Kwasi – TSHI

Strike the nose and the eyes shed tears – HAITIAN

Sympathy doesn't cure a sore – TSHI

The one who does it to himself is not cried over; it is the one to whom it is done who receives sympathy – NDEBELE

When someone is crying, your crying helps her – TSHI

When the eye weeps, the nose also becomes wet – DUALA

If you know what hurts yourself you know what hurts others – MALAGASY

T

If you meet an old man with a stick don't ask or comment about age –
UGANDAN

TACT

Do not call on your landlord if you have not paid your rent – **SWAHILI**

Don't look at a torn dress – **MALAGASY**

He who is a latecomer to a dance should not suggest a song - it might already have been sung – **GBANDE**

I address those below, but I mean those above – **UGANDAN**

If the hunter comes from the bush carrying mushrooms, you don't ask him how the hunting went – **TSHI**

Never count toes in the presence of a person with nine toes – **NIGERIAN**

One does not slaughter a calf before its mother's eyes – **NANDI**

The mouth must not relate everything the eyes see – **YORUBA**

Where you are not invited: you should avoid being there – **HAYA**

THEFT

A thief and darkness are friends – SHONA

'I entered and did not take' will not save a thief – HAUSA

If you steal an egg today, you'll steal an ox tomorrow – HAITIAN

It is my father's so let me take it, it is my mother's so let me take it, this brings a child to stealing – TSHI

One should see with one's eye, never with one's hand – GREBO

Stealing is done with courage – TSHI

Taking without admitting is theft – IGBO

[The] medicine of the thief is trouble – SUKUMA

Thieves take their own choice – TSWANA

When you catch a thief, he will say that it is his first time – IGBO

If you are teaching yourself to steal, teach yourself to run – SUKUMA

Stealing, not poverty, is disgraceful – TSHI

TEARS

New tears bring old ones back to memory – GANDA

Nothing dries faster than tears – HAITIAN

Tears fall according to the degree of grief – IGBO

The tears of one who loves you will come even from a bad eye – SWAHILI

To weep does ease the heart – TSWANA

You do not cry with only one eye – IGBO

TEMPTATION

Debil a-tempt, but he no a-fo'ce – GUYANAN
The devil tempts, but he doesn't force.

Don't send your child to fetch meat if she likes it very much – UGANDAN

He who got drunk without a hangover will try again – UGANDAN

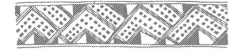

T

He steals a little, it is overlooked, then he steals much – **OVAMBO**

Ebery tief man know he own trade – **GUYANAN**
Every thief knows his own trade.

THOROUGHNESS

A trap without a bait catches nothing – **SWAHILI**

An animal does not hide itself and then leave its tail sticking out – **TSHI**

He who ties up a hyena should know how he is going to loose it – **HAUSA**

If you are going to twist thread make your knot so that it doesn't unwind – **HAUSA**

If you don't build your house well, you are afraid to sleep in it – **TSHI**

If you get ready to lay the trap, be also ready to tend it – **UGANDAN**

If you kill a snake, cut off its head – **IDOMA**

THOUGHT & THOUGHTLESSNESS

A person's thoughts are their kingdom – **TSONGA**

If thought does not pass on before as forethought, it subsequently returns as afterthought – **MONGO**

If you do not have thoughts you do not have understanding – **OVAMBO**

If yuh [your] head bad, yuh whole body bad – **BAJAN**

It is the mind which sees, the eye sees not – **HAUSA**

Monkey see, monkey do – **CREOLE (BELIZE)**

Taking thought is strength – **IGBO**

The heart that does not think utters foolishness – **GANDA**

The thinker is the knower – **MAMPRUSSI**

Thinking is wealth – **SWAHILI**

Thought breaks the heart – **EFIK**

To change one's mind is not a crime – **TSWANA**

You become old in your body, but you are still young in your mind – **GANDA**

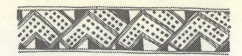

T

THREATS

The hissing of the snake is more effective than the braying of the donkey – ANCIENT EGYPTIAN

A threat and a fight are not equal – MONGO

I am not refused [passage] by the dog which is barking – KAMBA

The angry eyes of the frog don't prevent the cows from drinking – SUKUMA

Thundering is not raining – KIKUYU

TIME

'In time, 'twenty years hence' becomes 'tomorrow' – YORUBA

Time a-go [a]'way, but he no a-come back – GUYANAN

Time is a tutor – SWAHILI

Time longer dan [than] rope – JAMAICAN

To have time is to waste time – UGANDAN

When time is left out, time is found – IGBO

TIMELINESS

A twig is bent while still supple – UGANDAN

Choose your fellow traveller before you start on your journey – HAUSA

It is better to search for a black goat before it is dark – IGBO

It's not enough to run, you must (also) start on time – HAITIAN

On time is greater than being out first – MAMPRUSSI

Put out the fire while it is small – HAUSA

Strike the iron while it is still hot – SWAHILI

That which one sees in the daytime one need not seek with torches – EWE

The [decorative] marks on the mud wall are made at the same time as the wall – HAUSA

The dog doesn't shake its head until it's out of the water – BURJI

The rodent failed to fight when it should and expressed regret when it got to the market [i.e. for its carcass to be sold] – YORUBA

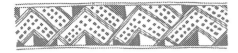 **T**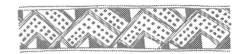

To escape a veld [pasture-land or unenclosed country] fire, flee when it is still far away – **SHONA**

Use your clay while it is wet – **SWAHILI**

What grew crooked when young cannot be straightened later – **GANDA**

When a lion eats a bad person and it is not killed, tomorrow it will eat a good person – **LOZI**

You should mend a hole in a likishi costume when it is still small – **LUVALE**

TIT-FOR-TAT

A tormentor is training his victims in harshness – **NIGERIAN**

As one plans for another, so god will plan for her – **IGBO**

As one is walking, so she is met – **YORUBA**

He who sells sand as salt will get stone as money – **YORUBA**

He who uncovers the affairs of another is one who will be uncovered – **ANCIENT EGYPTIAN**

Help the one who helps you – **SWAHILI**

'Hold back your dog, and I'll hold back my stick – **HAITIAN**

'If a child pretends to be dead, we pretend to bury him – **TSHI**

If a thousand people are deceiving you to catch you, you also deceive a thousand in running away from them – **TSHI**

If you consider your friend to be an animal he considers you to be shit – **TSHI**

Look for it and it will look for you – **OVAMBO**

Tief from tief mek Garamighty laugh – **GUYANAN**
A thief stealing from a thief makes God almighty laugh.

The light you brought to recognize your visitor, it is by the same light that the visitor recognizes the owner of the house – **IGBO**

Tit for tat and buttah [butter] for fat, you kill me dog I kill yuh [your] cat – **BAJAN**

Tit-for-tat has no bitterness – **KIKUYU**

To call in a bad mood...brings about a moody reply – **OROMO**

You make believe die, I make believe bury you – **HAITIAN**

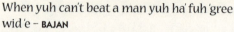

T

TOGETHERNESS & AGREEMENT

Cleverness and stupidity go together – **OVAMBO**

If two people set a trap together they go to see [visit] it together – **TWI**

Pig and mud go together – **SHONA**

See me an' live wid me da two different t'ing – **CREOLE (BELIZE)**
'See me' and 'live with me' are two different things.

We ate the sweet together, then bear thou even with the bitter – **SWAHILI**

You want paradise but not death – **FULANI**

People often agree in words but not in judgement – **KIKUYU**

To agree together is to make progress – **SUKUMA**

Two people in accord are stronger than eight who disagree – **SWAHILI**

When minds are one, what is far comes near – **SWAHILI**

When yuh can't beat a man yuh ha' fuh 'gree wid 'e – **BAJAN**
When you can't beat a man you have to agree with him.

TRADITION

Country tu'n [turns], but me haat [heart] no tu'n – **GUYANAN**
The country turns [changes], but my heart doesn't turn.

Old Used-To-Do-It-This-Way don't help none today – **AFRICAN-AMERICAN**

'This-is-how-it-is-usually-done' does not make people progress – **EWE**

The old arrow is a model for the craftsman making a new one – **TWI**

The young cannot teach tradition to the old – **YORUBA**

TRAINING

A child grows as it is raised – **SUKUMA**

Dog says that it is by biting that it makes its teeth strong – **IGBO**

T
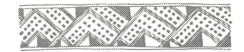

To bring up children by spoon-feeding will breed lazy ones – **SHONA**

A sharp knife is [one] that has been sharpened – **KIKUYU**

No one is a blacksmith at birth – **OVAMBO**

What is not sharpened does not cut – **SWAHILI**

The vulture's baby eats dung because of poor home training – **TSHI**

TRAVEL

The person who travels without aim is not like one who sits without aim, for the traveller usually picks up something – **SWAHILI**

It is the eye which has travelled that is clever – **MAASAI**

A person knows where they came from but not where they are going – **OVAMBO**

Much travelling teaches how to see – **UGANDAN**

One does not arrive early in the morning at a far-away place.[i.e. it takes time] – **OVAMBO**

One who does not move about knows very little of happenings – **HAYA**

Starting early doesn't mean a thing; it's knowing how to get there that counts – **HAITIAN**

The more you travel, the more poisonous snakes you will meet – **NAMIBIAN**

The questioner does not lose his way, but his secret is discovered – **HAUSA**

The traveller can tell all she has seen on his journey but she can't explain it all – **TSHI**

The very tall tree says that it sees far away; when you travel, you see far more than it – **HAITIAN**

Travel makes one see – **TSONGA**

Travelling means finding – **UGANDAN**

We go quickly where we are sent when we take interest in the journey – **WOLOF**

TRIAL

And come, pass by this rock, so we may know that you are a pilot – **SWAHILI**

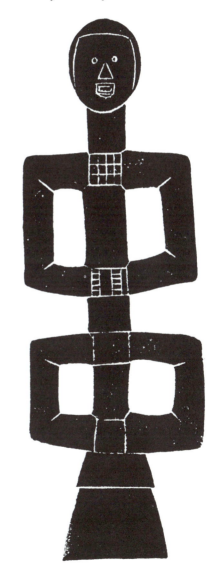

Try you' fre' in small ting, use him in great –
JAMAICAN
Try [i.e. test] your friend in a small thing, [then] use him in a great thing.

You want fe know if mauger darg hab teet',
draw him tail – **JAMAICAN**
You want to know if the dog has teeth, draw [i.e. pull] his tail.

Your husband's faithfulness is tested when
you are away – **UGANDAN**

TROUBLE

A penny buys troubles that doubloons
[Spanish gold coins] cannot cure –
TRINIDADIAN

A person won't be aware of troubles in the
water while remaining on the bank –
MAMPRUSSI

Don'[t] trouble trouble till trouble trouble
you – **BAJAN**

Fearing trouble won't make a strong person
– **MAMPRUSSI**

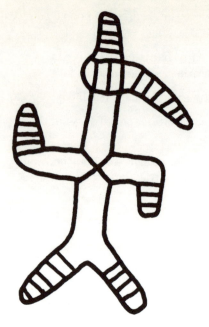

One who blockades a leopard will have
trouble – **YORUBA**

He who is the cause of his own troubles
never comes to the end of them: but he
who is troubled by others does – **KIKUYU**

Rather than eat that which is sweet and
have trouble, would I eat that which lacks
sweetness in peace – **HAUSA**

When someone's trouble has come,
someone else's trouble is on the way – **TSHI**

When trouble is coming, I prevent it, and
when it is entangled, I disentangle it. Which
of these two do you prefer? I prefer, when it
is coming, I prevent it – **TSHI**

She who is troubled by having property is
better of than she who is troubled by
poverty – **KIKUYU**

If you look for trouble you will not miss it –
MAASAI

It is no good steering clear of trouble
yourself if you let another draw you in –
HAUSA

It is troubles that take you far – **MAASAI**

Keep looking through the hedge and finally you'll scare up something that's sleeping [i.e. a snake] – **SUKUMA**

Satan trouble we when us trouble him – **JAMAICAN**

The chameleon says keep away from trouble and trouble keeps away from you – **MAMPRUSSI**

Trouble an' sea no gat no back doo' – **GUYANAN**
Trouble and the sea have got no back door.

Trouble come [u]'pon horseback, it go 'way 'pon foot – **GUYANAN**

'Trouble is afraid of the beard (an adult) – **TSHI**

Trouble mek puss run up prickly pear – **JAMAICAN**
Trouble makes the cat run up the prickly pear tree.

Trouble neva mek eself – **CREOLE (BELIZE)**
Trouble never makes himself.

Trouble worse dan [than] death – **BAJAN**

What has struck your home won't forget the way in – **UGANDAN**

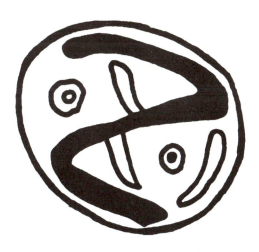

When trouble come, he no blow 'e [his] shell – **GUYANAN**

Trouble which you brought upon yourself is your own burden – **TSONGA**

Better is bread when the mind is at ease than riches with troubles – **ANCIENT EGYPTIAN**

TRUST & DISTRUST

A liar doesn't announce the enemy – **UGANDAN**

Befriend many but trust few – **UGANDAN**

He who does not trust others cannot be trusted – **SWAHILI**

He who disappoints another is unworthy to be trusted – **YORUBA**

Pay to-day, [obtain] trus'[t] tomorrow – **JAMAICAN**

There's danger in having too much trust – **HAITIAN**

Trust what you see – **SWAHILI**

De same tongue dat buy yuh [you] does sell yuh – **BAJAN**

If two people set a trap together, they also go to check it together – **TSHI**

Telling the truth can dig a grave – SURINAMESE

Telling the truth is no disgrace – SWAHILI

The truth hurts – HAITIAN

There can be no deceit in telling the truth – TSHI

There is not so much truth that it should be lessened by falsehood – TSHI

Truth is like sugar cane: even if you chew it for a long time, it is still sweet – MALAGASY

Truth reaches the market and becomes unsaleable; falsehood is in ready demand – YORUBA

Rogues do not buy from one another – ZULU

The animal which can't climb a tree should not trust [its] money to a monkey – KONGO

The robber does not desire a comrade to carry his knapsack for him – HAITIAN

She that sends children means to follow them – OROMO

TRUTH & TRUTHFULNESS

Bitter truth is better than sweet falsehood – SWAHILI

Children and fools speak the truth – OROMO

Dog don't get mad when you says he's a dog – AFRICAN-AMERICAN

Don't swear that you'll always speak the truth, just speak it – SUKUMA

He who says how many he has killed must tell you their names – UGANDAN

One who tells the truth makes no mistakes – SWAHILI

When you speak the truth in stating a case, the matter is quickly settled – TSHI

Telling someone the truth is not offending him – HAITIAN

U

A good looking person will not give birth to handsome children according to her will – **TSONGA**

Sick man no kyar, wha' doctor kyar? – **JAMAICAN**
The sick man doesn't care, why should the doctor care.

The fish on the grill is not afraid of burning – **HAITIAN**

The goat's business is not the sheep's affair – **MARTINIQUE**

How enjoyable the battle which doesn't affect you! – **UGANDAN**

UNITY & DISUNITY

A white dog does not bite another white dog – **KIKUYU**

Combination is stronger than witchcraft – **HAITIAN**

One stick can be broken but not a bundle of them – **SWAHILI**

Sticks in a bundle are unbreakable – **BONDEI**

The two broken halves will make one whole – **OROMO**

UNCONCERN

A dead body cannot smell itself – **IGBO**

A red hot pepper in another man's garden can never burn the tongue – **KIKUYU**

Cow no bisness [business] in a horse-play – **JAMAICAN**

If it has not happened to you, sleep – **TSHI**

It is all the same to a hen what rubber it eats, for it does not eat rubber at all – **HAUSA**

Unity is strength, division is weakness – **SWAHILI**

When minds are the same, that which is far off will come nigh – **SWAHILI**

A boat doesn't go forward if each one is rowing their own way – **SWAHILI**

People who have no unity are conquered with one club – **KIKUYU**

U

When two darg fight fe one bone, anoder darg run away wid i' – JAMAICAN
When two dogs fight for one bone, another dog runs away with it.

THE UNKNOWN

A woman knows not whether she will see tomorrow – EFIK

A womb is an indiscriminate container, it bears a thief and a witch – SHONA

Aiming does not mean hitting the target – GIRIAMA

The tortoise says that he is dancing superbly but because of his shell people cannot tell how well he is dancing – EWE

You can say how old you are, but you can't tell how much longer you're going to live – HAITIAN

You know what you're leaving, but you don't know what you're going to find – HAITIAN

USE & USEFULNESS

Betta fe ride ass dat carry you dan horse dat t'row you – JAMAICAN
Better to ride an ass that carries you than a horse that throws you.

Dutty [dirty] water wi'[ll] put out fire – JAMAICAN

If one could not make use of gold dust, then it would merely be called sand – ASHANTI

If you haven't good water, don't throw the bad water away – MAMPRUSSI

It is better to own one useful article than having many useless articles – HAYA

Lilly [little] water kill big fire – JAMAICAN

The overused pot ends up in pieces – UGANDAN

The use of fine clothes is the wearing of them – HAUSA

Where there is more than enough, more than enough is wasted – SOUTHERN AFRICA

You do not pour away the water you have in your pot because it is going to rain – EWE

USELESSNESS

A bad nose is one which can't smell – UGANDAN

It's a thing to be looked at only, like a bitter apple – SHONA

Somet'in' wha no' wut wile gies de most trouble – JAMAICAN
Something that's not worthwhile gives the most trouble.

The fruit that cannot be eaten has no use – BORAN

The parrot said a thousand things but none was of any use – IGBO

When the lock of a gun is out of order it (the gun) and a stick are just alike – ASHANTI

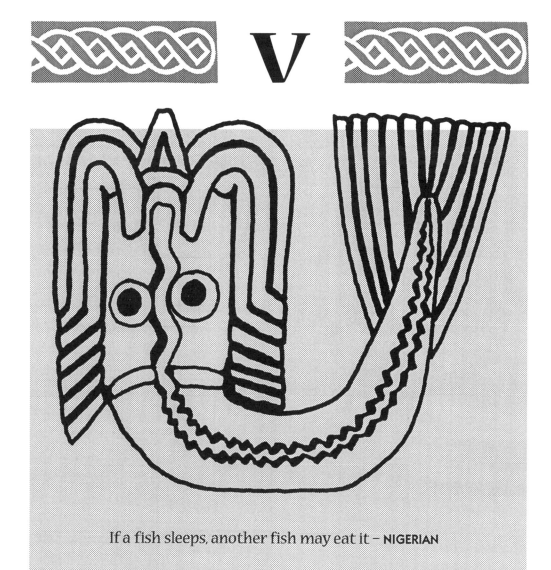

V

If a fish sleeps, another fish may eat it – NIGERIAN

VALUE

The parrot says valuable things are not picked up from the road but are brought with prices – IGBO

A rich man and his wealth, a poor woman and her child, they are equally inseparable, or devoted – SWAHILI

Good sometin' easy fe fling 'way, but hard fe pick up – JAMAICAN
A good (some)thing is easy to fling away, but hard to pick up.

What a fowl runs after under the rain is important to the fowl – IGBO

One often does not see what treasures are in her own backyard – HAITIAN

VANITY

Wild grass growing amongst beans thinks, 'I am a bean too.' – SHONA

A blind person does not worry over the loss of a looking-glass – HAUSA

VICISSITUDE

Daag [dog] walk [u]'pon dead lion – GUYANAN

De bridge between laughin' and cryin' no [isn't] long – JAMAICAN

She who laughs on Friday will cry on Sunday – LOUISIANA

He who passes you in the morning, you will pass him in the evening – GANDA

The one who starts well ends badly – ZULU

If you hear the drum sounds sweet, you can be sure it is near to the time it will split – HAUSA

Na [not] all man a-cou'tin' [a-courting] a-married – GUYANAN
Not every man who goes courting ends up married.

The agreeable taste does not live forever on the lip – KAMBA

What you push away from you today with your foot, you will pick up tomorrow with your hand – MARTINIQUE

While I was crying, you were laughing; I returned, and you were crying – MONGO

VICTORY & DEFEAT

Not all victories are enduring – HAITIAN

Being defeated and dying are the same – MAASAI

If you do not try you cannot win – OVAMBO

One who has taken refuge has surrendered – SHONA

The one who is defeated through truth does not come back – KIKUYU

VIGILANCE

Better see somet[h]in'[g] before sometin' see you – JAMAICAN

Rat does fuhget [forget] but not trap – BAJAN

The hunting dog doesn't sleep over the leopard's den – EWE

'If you don't use Saturday to keep watch on the road, you will use Sunday to run away – TSHI

When the chickens are sleeping, the hawk is keeping watch – HAITIAN

W

War begets no good offspring – MONGO

WAR

An only son is not known in the battle line – MONGO

It is they who have not died in war that start it – KIKUYU

De [the] soldier's blood, de general's name – JAMAICAN

The relations of a coward laugh: but those of a mighty fighter wail – GANDA

The armed man has no war – BONDEI

The mother of the brave wept, the mother of the timid laughed – GIRIAMA

You go to war slowly – TSHI

WARNING

A roaring lion does not catch any animal – ACHOLI

Barkin'[g] save a bitin' – JAMAICAN

Give the warning: some will survive – UGANDAN

No one has a dream showing where he will be killed and then goes there – TSHI

No trap was ever set whilst the birds were looking on – NDEBELE

When you see ole lady run, no ax wha' de matter, run too – JAMAICAN
When you see the old lady run, don't ask what's the matter, run too.

199

W

The lame person looks on while the stick is cut to beat them – HAUSA

The weakness of the strong is the strength of the weak – SWAHILI

When your guns are few, your words are few – TSHI

Darg [dog] bark nebber [never] frighten moon – JAMAICAN

The curse of the chicken does not reach the kite – SWAHILI

WEALTH & THE WEALTHY

A beggah beggin' from a beggah will nevah get rich – BAJAN
A beggar begging from a beggar will never get rich.

A fool owned many cows: they [i.e. people] never called him fool – TSWANA

A poor mulatto is a black; a rich black is a mulatto – HAITIAN

A rich man's breaking of wind is odourless – KIKUYU

WEAKNESS

A weak person goes where he is smiled at – HERERO

Are you a flag - to follow every breeze? – SWAHILI

He who asks a weak man for something, asks whilst taking it – GANDA

One who is younger than you strikes you with the stick you carry – HAYA

It a poor ting dat can' mash ant – JAMAICAN
It's a poor thing that can't mash [destroy] an ant.

It is a weak bird that wakes up early to look for food – NIGERIAN

One without strength laughs at [an] insult to his father – MAMPRUSSI

The weakest is always in the wrong – MARTINIQUE

The weakling drinks muddied water. [i.e. after others have drunk first] – KIKUYU

The hornless one associates with the one with horns – KIKUYU

W

Competent by inheritance, incompetent by character – **HAUSA**

Here flesh, there bone.[riches & poverty] – **SUKUMA**

If you are not rich, people don't value what you say – **TSHI**

Let an orphan get rich and she will find relatives – **UGANDAN**

One who has family and friends is richer than one who has money – **AFRICAN**

Riches are like a snake: it doesn't love only one place – **TSHI**

Side with snakes, not with the rich – **SHONA**

To be rich is due to sweat – **SHONA**

Wealth despises knowledge – **HAITIAN**

Wealth takes charge of its owner – **ANCIENT EGYPTIAN**

When a person is wealthy, they may wear whatever old clothes they like – **TSHI**

When han'[d] full him hab [have] plenty company – **BAHAMIAN**

When one is boasting of riches, they should endeavour also to tell of the source of these riches – **IGBO**

WILLINGNESS & UNWILLINGNESS

A de willin' harse dem saddle mos' – **JAMAICAN**
It's the willing horse they saddle most.

If the ear were an eye I would close it (i.e. I do not wish to hear) – **EFIK**

Send a boy where he wants to go and you'll see his best pace – **HAUSA**

The volunteer is worth ten pressed men – **HAUSA**

A choose [chosen] burden nebber [never] felt – **JAMAICAN**

WISDOM

A long life brings wisdom – **HAITIAN**

Anything that needs [to] be known can be understood by a wise person – **YORUBA**

Be unable to handle an axe, but don't be unable to handle instruction – **SUKUMA**

The termite is wise, and it uses its wisdom to build; the snake is wise and it uses its wisdom to be cruel; the bee is wise and it uses its wisdom to produce honey – YORUBA

The wise person who is not taught is not wise – KIKUYU

Those killed by lack of wisdom are numerous. Those killed by wisdom do not amount to anything – YORUBA

Wisdom is not like gold which should be kept in a safe – TWI

Wisdom outweighs strength – KIKUYU

WOMEN

A woman who starts to oppose her husband has found a place to go to – GANDA

Cattle can be inherited; a human being (woman) will choose for herself – SHONA

Handsome 'ooman [woman], handsome rogue – JAMAICAN

De wises'[t] man sometime fool – JAMAICAN

Even a wise person needs advice – SWAHILI

Foolishness often precedes wisdom – KONGO

She who has been advised is wise – KIKUYU

She who possesses much wisdom, has it in her heart; she who has little, has it on her lips – GANDA

It is not 'wisdom I have of myself'; wisdom is being told – LAMBA

It is through other people's wisdom that we learn wisdom; a single person's understanding does not amount to anything – YORUBA

Nobody is born wise – KIKUYU

One can never be too wise – HAITIAN

One who receives instructions will be wise – SWAHILI

Rebuke the wise man and he will like you – NZIMA

The eyes of a wise person see through you – HAYA

W

Very few males are as kind to children as females. It is the females who recall the labour pains – **HAYA**

WORDS

They catch an ox by its horns, they catch a man by his words – **TSONGA**

A cruel word is a wound of the heart; it does not heal, and even if it heals, the scar never departs – **SWAHILI**

A multitude of words cloaks a lie – **HAUSA**

A nice word is better than a nice mattress – **OROMO**

A word that when spoken you would wish back, let it remain unspoken in your head – **TSHI**

An offensive word hurts more than a flesh wound – **TSHI**

Anything is good enough to eat; but every word is not good enough to be spoken – **GUYANAN**

Beautiful words don't necessarily express true sentiments – **HAITIAN**

Fair words buy horses on credit – **TRINIDADIAN**

Fair words don'[t] prevent wrong doin'[g] – **BAJAN**

No matter how numerous, words don't break bones – **UGANDAN**

The words are the odour of the heart – **KIKUYU**

Words are not the same as wisdom – **TSHI**

Words in the heart have to be spoken before they satisfy – **TSWANA**

A good word removes anger – **GA**

WORK

A crooked stick makes us know (i.e. betrays) the carpenter – **OJI**

A person always breaking off from her work never finishes anything – **EFIK**

Do not be ashamed of honest work – **TWI**

Faada wo'k picknie spen' – **GUYANAN**
Father works, child spends.

Firewood will not collect itself – **NAMIBIAN**

If the kernels are not finished, the jaw will not rest – **IGBO**

Mout'[h] eat, back pay – GUYANAN

Perspire to eat – MAMPRUSSI

Sow when you dislike, you will reap when you like – HAUSA

The banana-bunch you have worked for is sweeter than the one you got for nothing – GANDA

The cat wants groundnuts: why is it that it did not hoe? – MAMPRUSSI

The earth provides for those who nourish it. [i.e. farmers] – YORUBA

The war of the stomach is fought and won with the hoe – SUKUMA

The work one imposed on oneself is never impossible – KIKUYU

To till the land is to love oneself – AFRICAN

What people get by hard work they don't get for their neighbours – TSHI

What went into the belly yesterday is not in the mouth today – EWE

When the work is a failure the worker feels shame – MONGO

If you want to eat in the evening, you have to work during the day – HAITIAN

Is not poor work good play? – SWAHILI

No sweet without sweat – UGANDAN

Riches are like perspiration: if you rest, they dry up – GANDA

Work hurts – HAITIAN

Work is good provided you do not forget to live – SOUTHERN AFRICA

Work that can be finished in one day is not real work – TSHI

THE WORLD

She who is not taught by her mother will be taught by the world – SWAHILI

One must come out of one's house to begin learning – AFRICAN

The outside world breeds in us little things like itself – TSONGA

Y

Elders see and keep silent, but to see and talk
are signs of the young – IGBO

YOUTH

If youthful arrogance were wealth, every
one of us would have been wealthy – TSHI

The money that a young person earns for
the first time is lavished in buying
unimportant things – YORUBA

The young bull mounts the cows from the
head – KIKUYU

Ethnic groups

Acholi: Kenya, Uganda
African
African-American: USA
Amharic: Ethiopia
Ancient Egyptian: Africa
Angass: Nigeria
Ashanti: Ghana
Bahamian: Bahamas
Bajan: Barbados
Bambara: Mali
Bantu: Southern Africa
Basa: Liberia
Bemba: Zaire, Zambia,
    Zimbabwe
Bini: Nigeria
Bondei: Kenya
Boran: Kenya
Bura: Nigeria
Burji: Kenya
Chagga: Tanzania
Chopi: Mozambique, South
    Africa
Creole (Belize): Central America
Duala: Cameroon
Efik: Nigeria
Etsako: West Africa
Ewe: Ghana, Benin, Togo
Fipa: Tanzania
Fulani: Burkina Faso, Cameroon,
    Gambia, Guinea, Mali Nigeria,
Senegal
Fulfulde (aka Fulani, Fulbe:
    see Fulani)
Ga: Ghana
Galla: Kenya, Ethiopia
Ganda: Uganda
Gbande: Liberia
Gio: Liberia
Giriama: Kenya
Gogo: Tanzania
Grebo: Liberia
Gurage: Ethiopia
Kisii: Kenya
Guyanan/British Guiana: Guyana,
    South America
Haitian: Haiti
Hausa: Niger, Nigeria
Haya: Tanzania
Ho: Togo
Idoma: Nigeria
Igbo: Nigeria

Ila: Zambia
Iteso: Uganda
Jabo: Liberia
Jamaican: Jamaica
Jukun: Nigeria
Kalenjin: Kenya
Kamba: Kenya, Tanzania
Kanuri, Kanuri/Bornu: Chad,
    Niger, Nigeria
Kaonde: Zambia
Kikuyu: Kenya
Kipsigis: Kenya
Kongo: Angola, Congo, DR Congo
Kru: Liberia, Ivory Coast
Kuranko/Koranko: Sierra Leone
Kuria: Kenya
Kweli: Cameroon
Lamba: DR Congo, Zambia
Louisiana, Louisiana Creole: USA
Lozi: Zambia
Luo: Kenya, Tanzania
Luvale: Zambia
Luyia: Kenya, Uganda
Maasai: Kenya, Tanzania
Malagasy: Madagascar
Mamprussi: Burkina Faso
Marakwet: Kenya
Martinique: Martinique,
    (Caribbean)

Mauritian: Mauritius
Mende: Sierra Leone
Mongo: DR Congo
Namibian: Namibia
Nandi: Kenya
Ndebele: Zimbabwe
Ndonga: Namibia
Nigerian: Nigeria
Nkundu: DR Congo
Nupe: Nigeria
Nyang: Cameroon
Nyanja: Zambia, Malawi,
    Mozambique, Zimbabwe
Nyika: Kenya
Nzima: Ghana
Oji: Ghana
Oromo: Ethiopia, Kenya
Ovaherero: Namibia
Ovambo: Angola, Namibia
Pedi: South Africa
Rwanda: Burundi, Rwanda,
    Tanzania, Uganda
Sherbro: Sierra Leone
Shona: Mozambique, Zimbabwe
Sotho: Botswana, Lesotho,
    South Africa
Sukuma: Tanzania
Surinamese: Surinam, South
    America
Swahili: East Africa (inc. Kenya,
    Tanzania, Somalia)
Tamashek (Tuareg): Algeria,
    Mali, Niger
Temne: Sierra Leone
Thonga: Zimbabwe, South Africa
Tiv : Cameroon, Nigeria
Tonga: Zambia
Trinidadian: Trinidad
Tshi: Ghana
Tshwa
Tsonga: Mozambique
Tswana: Botswana, South Africa
Tumbuka-Kamanga: Malawi
    Twi: Ghana
Ugandan: Uganda
Vai: Liberia, Sierra Leone
West Indian: Caribbean
Wolof: Gambia, Senegal
Xhosa: South Africa
Yoruba: Benin, Nigeria, Togo
Zulu: South Africa

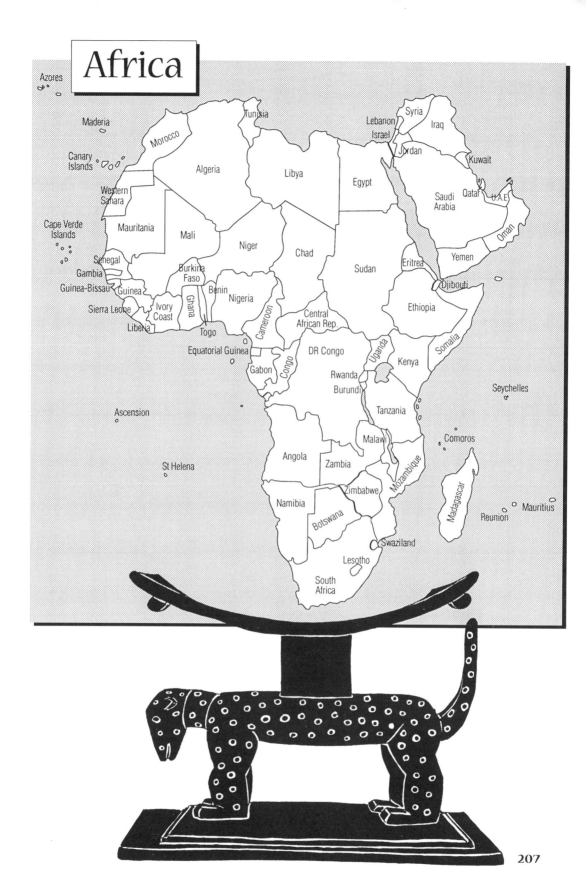

Africa

Azores

Maderia

Canary
Islands

Cape Verde
Islands

Western
Sahara

Senegal

Gambia

Guinea-Bissau

Sierra Leone

Liberia

Morocco

Algeria

Mauritania

Mali

Burkina
Faso

Guinea

Ivory
Coast

Ghana

Togo

Benin

Tunisia

Libya

Niger

Nigeria

Equatorial Guinea

Cameroon

Gabon

Congo

Chad

Central
African Rep.

DR Congo

Rwanda

Burundi

Egypt

Sudan

Uganda

Tanzania

Lebanon
Israel

Syria

Jordan

Saudi
Arabia

Eritrea

Djibouti

Ethiopia

Kenya

Iraq

Kuwait

Qatar

U.A.E.

Oman

Yemen

Somalia

Seychelles

Comoros

Ascension

St Helena

Angola

Zambia

Malawi

Mozambique

Madagascar

Reunion

Mauritius

Namibia

Zimbabwe

Botswana

Swaziland

Lesotho

South
Africa

207

Bibliography

Abraham, Captain R C, The Principles of Idoma, *Published by The Author, 1935*

Akrofi, Clement, Twi Mmebusem (Twi Proverbs), *Presbyterian Book Depot, Kumasi, Macmillan and Co Ltd, St Martin'S Street London, 1962*

Anderson, Izett, and Frank Cundall, Jamaica Proverbs and Sayings, *Institute of Jamaica, Kingston, 1972 (First Published London, 1910)*

Areje, Raphael Adekunle, Yoruba Proverbs, *Daystar Press, Ibadan, Nigeria, 1985*

Bai–Sharka, Abou, Temne Names And Proverbs, *People's Educational Association of Sierra Leone, 1986*

Barra, G, 1000 Kikuyu Proverbs, *The East African Literature Bureau, Macmillan and Co Ltd, London, 1960*

Basden, G T, Among The Ibos of Nigeria, *University Publishing Co, Academy Press Ltd, Lagos, 1982 (First Publ. 1921)*

Bazinge, Dr J, Ibo Proverbs, *Published by the Author, Lagos, 1972*

Bigelow, John, Wit And Wisdom of The Haytians, *New York, Scribner & Armstrong, 1877*

Blackman, Margot, Bajan Proverbs, *Caribbean Graphic Production Ltd, 1982*

Bloah, Charles, and George Herzog, Jabo Proverbs *from Liberia, Oxford University Press, 1936*

Bordinat, Philip, and Peter Thomas, Revealer of Secrets, *African Universities Press, Lagos, 1973*

Burdon, Sir John, and C E J Whitting, Hausa and Fulani Proverbs, Lagos, *Printed by the Government Printer, 1940*

Burton, Richard F, Wit and Wisdom from West Africa, *London, Tinsley Brothers, 1865*

Cagnolo, Fr C, The Akikuyu – Their Customs, Traditions and Folklore, *The Missionary Printing School, Nyeri, Kenya, 1933*

Champion, Selwyn, Racial Proverbs, *London George Routledge & Sons Ltd, 1938*

Christaller, G J, and Kofi Ron Lange, 3,600 Ghanian Proverbs (from the Asante and Fante Languages), *The Edwin Mellen Press, Lewiston, Queenston, Lampeter, 1990*

Cisternino, Fr Marius, The Proverbs of Kigezi and Ankole, *Museum Combonianum No 41, 1987*

Cotter, Fr George, Sukuma Proverbs, *Beezee Secretarial Services, Nairobi, Kenya, 1968*

Courlander, Harold, A Treasury of Afro–American Folklore, *Crown Publishers, Inc, New York, 1976*

Cullen, The Rev T, Notes on the Customs And Folklore on the Tumbuka–Kamanga, *Mission Press, Livingstonia, 1931*

Davids, Pauline Aduke, Ilulu Igbo – The Textbook of Igbo Proverbs, *Varsity Industrial Press, Onitsha, 1980*

Delano, Isaac, Yoruba Proverbs, Ibadan, *Oxford University Press, 1966*

Dennis, Benjamin, The Gbandes – A People of The Liberian Hinterland, *Nelson–Hall Company, Chicago, 1972*

Doke, Clement, Lamba Folklore, *The American Folklore Society, New York, 1927*

Dundas, Charles, Kilimanjaro and its People, *London, H. F. And G. Witherby, 1924*

Dunning, R G, Two Hundred and Sixty Four Zulu Proverbs, Idioms, Etc, *The Knox Printing And Publishing Co., Durban, S Africa, 1946*

Dzobo, N K, African Proverbs: Guide to Conduct (The Moral Value Of Ewe Proverbs), 2 Vols, *Waterville Publishing House Division of Presbyterian Book Depot, Ltd, Accra, 1975*

Eguchi, Paul Kazuhisa, Miscellany Of Maroua Fulfulde (Northern Cameroun), *Vol 1, Institute for the Study of Languages & Cultures of Asia and Africa, Tokyo, 1974*

Ellis, A B, The Ewe–Speaking Peoples of The Slave Coast of West Africa, *London, Chapman & Hall, 1890*

Ellis, A B, The Yoruba–Speaking Peoples of The Slave Coast of West Africa, *London, Chapman & Hall Ltd, 1894*

Fayo, 3,333 Proverbs in Haitian Creole – The 11th Romance Language, *Les Editions Fardin, Port–Au–Prince, Haiti, 1981*

Fletcher, Roland, Hausa Sayings and Folk–Lore, Henry Frowde, *Oxford University Press, 1912*

Faulkner, R O, William Kelly Simpson And Edward F Wente, The Literature of Ancient Egypt, *New Haven And London, Yale Univeersity Press, 1973*

Foulkes, H D, Angass Manual, *Kegan Paul, Trench, Truber & Co Ltd, London, 1915*

Ganly, Fr John C, Kaonde Proverbs, *Mission Press, Ndola, 1987*

Gichuke, Alexander And Esmee, Gikuyu Proverbs, Nairobi, *Oxford University Press, 1983*

Green, M M, And The Rev G E Igwe, Igbo Language Course, Book Iii: Dialogues, Sayings, Translations, Ibadan, *Oxford University Press, 1970*

Greene, Anthony, Hausa Ba Dabo Ba Ne, Ibadan, *Oxford University Press, 1966*

Hamutyinei, M, and A Plangger, Tsumo–Shumo: Shona Proverbial Lore And Wisdom, *Salisbury, Mambo Press, 1974*

Haskett, Edythe Rance, Grains of Pepper – Folktales from Liberia, *Abelard–Schuman, London, 1970*

Hearn, Lafcadio, Little Dictionary of Creole Proverbs, *Will H Coleman, New York, 1885*

Hinzen, Heribert, Frederick Bobor James, Jim Martin Sorie & Sheikh Ahmed Tejan Tamu Editors, Fishing In Rivers Of Sierra Leone – Oral Literature, *People's Educational Association Of Sierra Leone, Freetown, 1987*

Hollis, A C, The Masai – Their Language and Folklore, *Oxford, 1905*

Hollis, A C, The Nandi – Their Language and Folklore, *Oxford, 1909*

Ichie, Ndi and I N C Nwosu, Akwa Mythology and Folklore Origins of The Igbos, *Css Press, Lagos, 1983*

Jablow, Alta, An Anthology of West African Folklore, *Thames and Hudson, 1961*

Johnson, The Ven W P, Chinyanja Proverbs, *Smith Bros, 1922*

Junod, Henri, The Wisdom of the Tsonga–Shangana People, *Sasavona Publishers, Braamfontein, 1981*

Kabira, Wanjiku Mukabi, and Karega Mutahi, Gikuyu Oral Literature, *English Press Ltd, Kenya, 1988*

Kalugila, Leonidas, and Abdulaziz Lodhi, More Swahili Proverbs from East Africa, *Scandinavian Institute Of African Studies, Uppsala, 1980*

Kipury, Naomi, Oral Literature of the Maasai, *Heinemann Educational Books, Nairobi, Kenya 1983*

Koenig, Jean–Paul, Malagasy Customs and Proverbs, *Editions Naaman, Canada, 1984*

Koelle, The Rev S W, African Native Literature or Proverbs, Tales, Fables And Historical Fragments in the Kanuri or Bornu Language, London, *Church Missionary House, Salisbury Square, 1854*

Knappert, Jan, Namibia – Land and Peoples, Myths and Legends, E J Brill, *Leiden, 1981*

Knappert, Jan, Myths and Legends Of Botswana, Lesotho and Swaziland, E J Brill, *Leiden, 1985*

Knappert, Jan, Proverbs from the Lamu Archipelago and the Central Kenya Coast, Dietrich Reimer *Verlag, Berlin, 1986*

Kuusi, Matti, Ovambo Proverbs, Suomalainen Tiedeakatemia, *Helsinki, 1970*

Lawrance, J, The Iteso, *Oxford University Press, 1957*

Leslau, Wolf, Gurage Folklore, Franz Steiner Verlag Gmbh, *Wiesbaden, 1982*

Lichtheim, Miriam, Late Egyptian Wisdom Literature in the International Context, V*andenhoeck & Ruprecht, Gottingen, 1983*

Lindblom, Gerhard, Kamba Folklore, Vol Iii: Kamba Riddles, Proverbs and Songs, *Uppsala, 1934*

Lindfors, B, And O Owomoyela, Yoruba Proverbs, Ohio University *Centre for International Studies, Africa Program, 1973*

Macquitty, William, The Wisdom of The Ancient Egyptian, *Sheldon Press, London, 1978*

Meena, E, Misemo, 4 Vols, Transafrica Publishers Ltd, *Nairobi, 1975*

Merrick, Captain G, Hausa Proverbs, London, Kegan Paul, Trench, *Truber & Co. Ltd, 1905*

Migeod, Frederick, A View of Sierra Leone, Kegan Paul, Trench, *Truber & Co Ltd, 1926*

Molema, S, The Bantu Past And

Present, Edinburgh, *W. Green & Son Ltd, 1920*

Ndeti, K, Elements Of Akamba Life, *East African Publishing House, 1972*

Nestor, H B, 500 Haya Proverbs, East African Literature Bureau, *Kenya, 1977*

Njoku, John Eberegbulam, The Igbos Of Nigeria – Ancient Rites, Changes and Survival, African Studies Vol. 14, *The Edwin Mellen Press, Lewiston, Queenston, Lampeter, 1990*

Nyembezi, C L, Zulu Proverbs, Witwatersrand University Press, *Johannesburg, 1963*

Odaga, Asenath Bole, Yesterday's Today: The Study of Oral Literature, *Lake Publishers And Enterprises, Kenya, 1991*

Opoku, Kofi, Speak to the Winds, *Lothrop, Lee And Shepard Company, New York, 1975*

Orjii, Edward, 1,350 Igbo Proverbs, *Plateau Publishing Co. Ltd, Jos, 1984*

P'Bitek, Okot, Acholi Proverbs, *Heinemann Kenya Ltd, Nairobi, 1985*

Peek, Basil, 'Bahamian Proverbs,' *The Providence Press, Nassau, Bahamas, 1966*

Pelling, J N, Ndebele Proverbs, *Mambo Press in Association with The Rhodesia Literature Bureau, 1977*

Penfield, Joyce Okezie, Communicating with Quotes – *The Igbo Case, Greenwood Press, Westport, Connecticut and London, 1983*

Plaatje, Solomon, Sechuana Proverbs, London, *Kegan Paul, Trench, Truber & Co. Ltd, 1916*

Plissart, Xavier, Mamprussi Proverbs, Tervuren, Musée Royal De L'Afrique Centrale, 1983

Rattray, R Sutherland, Hausa Folklore, Customs, Proverbs, Etc, Vol Ii, Oxford at the *Clarendon Press, 1913*

Rattray, R Sutherland, Ashanti Proverbs, *Oxford, 1916*

Rikitu, Mengesha, Oromo Oral Treasure for a New Generation, *Top Print, London, 1992*

Roscoe, The Rev John, The Baganda – Their Customs and Beliefs, *Macmillan and Co Ltd,*

London, 1911

Rowling, The Rev Canon F, Tales of Sir Apollo – Uganda Folklore and Proverbs, *The Religious Tract Society, London, 1927*

Ruskin, E A, Mongo Proverbs and Fables, Bongandanga Congo Balolo *Mission Press, Belgian Congo, 1921*

St Lys, Odette, From A Vanished German Colony – A Collection Of Folklore, Folk Tales And Proverbs From South–West Africa, *London, 1916*

Scheven, Albert, Swahili Proverbs, *University Press Of America, 1981*

Speirs, James, The Proverbs of British Guiana, Demerara, *The Argosy Co, 1902*

Steere, Edward, Swahili Tales, *London, 1870*

Stiglmayr, Engelbert, Sayings Of Wisdom, *Wien, 1973*

Sumbwa, Nyambe, Zambian Proverbs, *Zpc Publications, Lusaka, 1993*

Taiwo, C Oladele, The King's Heir – Nigerian Folktales, Riddles and Proverbs, *London, Nelson, 1965*

Taylor, The Rev W E, African Aphorisms; or Saws from Swahili–Land, Society for Promoting Christian Knowledge, *London, 1891*

Theal, George Kaffir, Folklore, 2nd Edition, London, Swan, Sonnenschein, Le Bas & Lowrey, *Paternoster Square, 1886*

Thomas, Northcote W, Anthropological Report on the Ibo–Speaking Peoples of Nigeria, Part Vi – Proverbs, Stories, Tones in Ibo, *London, Harrison And Sons, 1914*

Wako, Daniel M, The Western Abaluyia and their Proverbs, *Kenya Literature Bureau, 1985*

Walser, Fr Ferdinand, Luganda Proverbs, *Dietrich Reimer Verlag, 1982*

Willis, Roy, There was a Certain Man – Spoken Art of the Fipa, *Oxford, 1978*

Wk, Swahili Notes Part 4 – Proverbs, Universities' *Mission Press, Zanzibar, 1899*

Young, C N, Creole Proverbs of Belize, *1980*

ABOUT THE AUTHOR

PATRICK IBEKWE was born on 13 August 1964 and educated at the London School of Economics (Honours Degree in Law, 1985), and the University of West England (Master of Science Degree in Information Technology, 1990) – he is currently studying for a Master of Science Degree in Public Policy and Public Administration at the LSE. He has worked since 1990 for the Department for Education and Employment in London, as a Higher Executive Officer. Patrick Ibekwe lives in London, and follows closely political and social developments in Nigeria, his family's country of origin.